The **Greek** Mama's Kitchen

The **Greek** **Mama's** Kitchen

Authentic homestyle recipes

Rosemary Barron

THUNDER BAY
P·R·E·S·S

San Diego, California

Thunder Bay Press

An imprint of the Advantage Publishers Group

5880 Oberlin Drive, San Diego, CA 92121-4794

www.thunderbaybooks.com

Library of Congress Cataloging-in-Publication Data

Barron, Rosemary.

The Greek mama's kitchen : authentic homestyle recipes / Rosemary Barron.

p. cm.

ISBN 1-59223-421-6

1. Cookery, Greek. I. Title.

TX723.5.G8B372 2005

641.59495--dc22

2005043070

Printed and bound in China.

1 2 3 4 5   09 08 07 06 05

Picture Credits:

The Anthony Blake Picture Library: pages 39, 42–43, 94–95 and 140–141 © Anthony Blake/Anthony Blake Picture Library; pages 122–123 © Martin Brigdale/Anthony Blake Picture Library; *Cephas*: pages 30–31 © Stockfood; page 34 © Stockfood; page 119 © Stockfood; *Corbis*: cover and endpapers © Jose Luis Pelaez, Inc./CORBIS; page 7 © John Heseltine/CORBIS; pages 10–11 © Ludovic Maisant/CORBIS; pages 108–109 © Adam Woolfitt/CORBIS; *Food Features*: pages 27, 70–71 and 105 © Food Features; *Getty Images*: page 9 © Benjamin F. Fink Jr./Foodpix/Getty Images; *StockFood*: pages 2 and 57 © Eising/www.stockfood.com; page 17 © Aurora Photos S.L./www.stockfood.com; page 45 © Moretto, Alberto/www.stockfood.com; page 79 © Silverman, Ellen/www.stockfood.com; page 92 ©Newedel, Karl/www.stockfood.com; page 112 © Studio Bonisolli/www.stockfood.com; page 132 © Plewinski, Antje/www.stockfood.com; page 144 © Feuz, Rolf/www.stockfood.com; page 153 © Iden, K./www.stockfood.com

Contents

Introduction

My kitchen is at the center of our home life, and it's the place I love to be. It's not a large kitchen, nor does it have much equipment, compared to kitchens I've seen in cities, but I can create dishes here that delight and sustain my family throughout the year.

My kitchen opens out onto a courtyard, which is shaded by an ancient fig tree on one side and by a beautiful vine on the other. Our wood-burning oven is just inside the courtyard gate, and next to it is a storage room in which I keep my preserves, pickles, cheeses, and yogurt, and hang my figs to dry. An enormous table occupies part of the courtyard—this is where we enjoy our meals together whenever we can.

Inside my kitchen, I have a large wooden table on which I make our breads, cakes, and pies. I have a stove, an oven, plenty of pots, strainers, and bowls, and three different sizes of *tapsi* (large round baking pans). My favorite kitchen tools are my two mortars—a large marble one that I use to make salates (see page 13) and a small wooden one for preparing herbs—and my *skafi*, a wooden trough that I use to mix and knead my bread dough.

Just beyond the courtyard is my kitchen garden. A short walk past our garden are our orchards, beehives, olive trees, and a small vineyard. During the winter I keep my six goats close to the kitchen garden so that I can easily feed them, but I tether them in the orchards during the rest of the year. My family has always kept goats. As a child, I didn't much like their strong smell and equally strong temperament, but I soon grew to love and appreciate the animals. Throughout the fall, winter, and spring, the goats give us plenty of milk for our cheeses. I make feta cheese with the whole milk, and I use its whey to make myzithra, a soft, fresh cheese. For yogurt, my family prefers the milder, sweet flavor of sheep's milk. So I barter with the village shepherd, trading our spare honey for milk from his large flock.

From my house, I can see the lower slopes of the Peloponnese mountains, where I gather my *horta* (wild greens), herbs for my teas, and snails. To reach the mountains, I cross a shallow river just as it flows out to the sea, and this is where I find the little shellfish I love to turn into mezes.

In my kitchen garden, I grow my favorite fresh herbs in great quantities—parsley, cilantro, thyme, chervil, dill, fennel, and rosemary. My garden is also ideal for growing vegetables, such as zucchini, eggplant, potatoes, carrots, cauliflower, peppers, spinach, asparagus, tomatoes, okra, salad greens—and more. Giant prickly artichokes grow on either side of the garden and act as walls to keep my goats where they belong—outside! I have a bay tree, two lemon trees, a large pomegranate tree, and a beautiful quince shrub along the south facing wall.

In my orchard, I grow apricots, pears, cherries, apples, and oranges. These fruit trees provide us with our favorite end to a meal—a platter of fresh fruit, just picked and still warm from the sun.

We also have many olive trees, for olives and olive oil are the staples of my kitchen. A few of our trees grow close to the river, and it's with the olives from these that we make our olive oil. The trees on the hillsides provide us with smaller, less fleshy, but more flavorful olives. We harvest our olives during the late fall. Our neighbors help us, just as we help them when their olives are ready to be gathered. I like to pick some olives very early in the harvest, just before their color changes to dark green. These young olives, which are still green when they are cured, are a perfect complement to artichokes and other flavors of spring, and to fish dishes such as taramosalata (a dip made from mullet roe). I cure most of our olives in brine, but some I cure in sea salt and oil. These become wrinkly and chewy, and make a delicious meze.

A lovely vine shades one side of our courtyard. During late summer, huge clusters of grapes hang down over our table. At the end of a meal, all I have to do is reach up and pluck off a bunch for everyone to enjoy. We also have a small vineyard, and we use the grapes grown here to make our wine. Every spring, I use some of the tender little leaves found at the top of the vine to make dolmadakia (see pages 26–28), and I preserve many more in brine, for use the rest of the year. During the summer, I use older leaves to protect and flavor my bakes (see pages 86–87). I like to make a sauce from the not-yet-ripened, sour-flavored little grapes and, later in the year, I gather ripe grapes to make petimezi (grape must), which I use to make a jellylike sweet treat, moustalevria, and to flavor rice puddings (see page 133), cakes, and cookies.

My husband and his friends make our wine in September. Until a few years ago, they stomped the grapes with their feet; these days they take the grapes to the local cooperative where they are weighed and transformed into wine, with an equivalent amount of wine returned to us. This works well for all of us, as stomping grapes can be backbreaking and time-consuming work. In the corner of my storehouse, I have a large clay pot that contains my vinegar—the remnants of the odd bottle of wine left over from a meal. It has a wonderful depth of flavor that I miss when I am away from home.

One of my greatest pleasures is to gather foods on the nearby hillsides, beach, and riverbanks, and from the fields and river estuary. Every spring, I pick mountain herbs—rigani (Greek oregano—a very pungent variety of the plant), sage, marjoram, and thyme—just before they flower, and I hang them in my storehouse to dry. I collect capers (unopened flower buds) from the pretty caper vines that cover our field walls to preserve in brine. I gather mint and watercress from the river's edge. I'm particularly happy when it rains, or rather, just after it rains—for it's at that moment I find the best snails and horta (wild greens).

For us, horta holds a very special meaning: it's one of the foods that has sustained us through bad times as well as good times. It's free—all we have to do is find it. My favorite horta is *rathikia* (wild chicory), which is at its bitter best in very early spring. I also love young arugula, *vlita* (amaranth greens, which are similar in flavor to water spinach), dandelion greens, and mustard greens. I use young, tender wild greens in raw salads, but older greens must be boiled to soften them. I add the greens to casseroles and soups, and use them in pies (see pages 116–117). In summer, when there is no rain, we have no horta, but during the fall, winter, and spring, I try to have a bowl of horta on the table at every meal.

Although I have a refrigerator, my kitchen life is controlled by the seasons. I create dishes from whatever vegetables are available that day, and I prefer to store food in the ways I learned when I was a child—I dry figs, salt olives, and fish, turn fruits into jams, and transform fresh bread into long-lasting rusks. Every day is a different day in my kitchen, and this is how I want it to be.

Chapter one
MEZES

Chickpea and Sesame Dip
Revithosalata

Lent is a time of year when I really have to think about the dishes I prepare for my family, as there are so many foods and ingredients we don't eat during that period! Red meats are off the menu, so I have to make sure we obtain plenty of protein from other sources. Chickpeas and tahini (a nutritious paste made from sesame seeds) serves my purpose well. Don't be tempted to use canned chickpeas—their flavor and texture are far inferior to dried peas. Revithosalata can easily be made in a food processor, and may be refrigerated in a covered container for up to two days.

SERVES: 6 to 8

1 cup chickpeas, covered by 3 inches of water and soaked 6 hours or overnight
1 tablespoon tahini paste (available in specialty food stores) ◆ 1 large clove garlic, chopped
Juice of 1 small lemon or to taste ◆ ½ cup extra-virgin olive oil or more to taste
Fine sea salt and finely cracked pepper to taste ◆ 1 teaspoon sumac
1 tablespoon dried Greek oregano, crumbled

◆

1 Drain the chickpeas and transfer to a large saucepan. Add water to cover by 3 inches. Bring to a boil, reduce the heat to low, cover, and simmer 40 minutes or until the chickpeas are soft. Drain over a bowl. Measure 1 cup cooking liquid and reserve; discard the remainder. Set aside a few chickpeas for garnish.

2 Place the tahini, garlic, half the lemon juice, 5 tablespoons of the olive oil, and a little salt and pepper in a food processor or blender bowl; pulse to mix. Add the chickpeas and half the reserved cooking liquid. With the machine running, gradually add the remaining reserved liquid and most of the olive oil; stop when the mixture is smooth and creamy. Taste and add more salt and pepper if desired. To thin the dip, gradually add a little water (or extra olive oil) until the desired consistency is reached. Transfer to a shallow serving bowl or platter.

3 In a small bowl, lightly whisk together the sumac, oregano, and the remaining lemon juice and olive oil. Pour this sauce over the revithosalata and garnish with the reserved chickpeas.

Eggplant Dip
Melitzanosalata

For the traditional mellow and smoky flavor we like for this dish, broil the eggplants before preparing the dip. If you have a few extra moments, you can create an even better flavor by pounding the eggplants in a mortar instead of pulsing them in a food processor.

SERVES: 6 to 8

4 small to medium eggplants
2 plump cloves garlic (or to taste), chopped ◆ Coarse sea salt to taste
2 tablespoons capers, rinsed and patted dry ◆ 4 green onions, white parts only, chopped
4 tablespoons chopped fresh flat-leaf parsley ◆ 1 tablespoon red wine vinegar or to taste
Finely cracked pepper to taste ◆ ¼ cup extra-virgin olive oil or to taste ◆ ½ teaspoon paprika

◆

1 Heat the broiler or grill.

2 Trim off the stem ends, and make 6 small slits in each eggplant. Broil on all sides until the skins scorch and the centers are soft, about 15 minutes.

3 When the eggplants are cool enough to handle, peel off and discard the skins. Place the flesh on a chopping board. Remove and discard as many of the seeds as possible, and gently squeeze the flesh between paper towels to remove excess moisture.

4 Place the garlic and a little salt in a mortar or small bowl. Using a pestle or wooden spoon,

pound the two ingredients together until they are well blended.

5 Place the capers, green onions, and half the parsley in a food processor bowl. Pulse until well mixed. Add the eggplant flesh, garlic mixture, vinegar, pepper, and salt. Pulse a few times, to mix. Still using the pulse switch, add the olive oil in a thin, steady stream; stop when well mixed, but not smooth. Taste, and add more salt, pepper, vinegar and/or olive oil if desired. Transfer to a bowl, cover tightly, and refrigerate for at least one hour.

6 To serve, sprinkle with paprika and the remaining parsley.

Yogurt and Cucumber Dip
Tsatsiki

Tsatsiki tastes especially good in the spring, when our yogurt is extra rich and creamy and our herb garden patch is thriving. Delicious as part of a meze table or as a side dish to grilled or fried meats, tsatsiki should always be served as soon as possible after its preparation, for it tends to become watery if stored.

SERVES: 6 to 8

1 large English cucumber, peeled
2 to 4 plump cloves very fresh garlic (to taste), chopped ◆ ½ teaspoon sea salt or to taste
2 cups strained yogurt ◆ Freshly ground pepper
2 tablespoons extra-virgin olive oil
6 tablespoons coarsely chopped fresh dill or 3 tablespoons fresh young mint leaves,
torn into small pieces at the last minute
A few sprigs of fresh dill or mint, for garnish

◆

1 Using a knife or grater, julienne the cucumber. Transfer to a colander and set a plate directly onto the cucumber to weight the slices. Set aside 30 minutes to drain.

2 Place the garlic and salt in a mortar or small bowl. Using a pestle or wooden spoon, pound the two ingredients together until they are well blended.

3 In a large bowl, combine the yogurt, pepper, and garlic mixture. Whisk in the olive oil.

4 Squeeze the cucumber between paper towels to remove as much moisture as possible. Add to the yogurt mixture with the chopped dill or the mint leaves. Stir to mix.

5 Transfer to a serving bowl or platter, and garnish with dill or mint sprigs.

Red Cheese Dip

Tyrosalata

If you ever have some spare feta cheese on hand, this dip is a good way to make use of it. Serve tyrosalata with bowls of olives.

SERVES: 6 to 8

1 medium red bell pepper ◆ ¾ cup cottage cheese, drained
1 cup feta cheese, drained and crumbled
¼ cup extra-virgin olive oil ◆ Large pinch of cayenne pepper
Freshly ground pepper to taste ◆ 2 tablespoons chopped chives

◆

1 Roast the pepper. Using tongs, hold the pepper over an open flame or place on a hot grill, turning until blistered and blackened on all sides. Transfer to a paper bag or a bowl; close the bag or cover the bowl with plastic wrap, and set aside to cool.

2 Using your fingers, rub off and discard the skin from the blackened pepper, and discard the core and seeds (but don't rinse the pepper—water will spoil its flavor). Cut it into small pieces and place it in a food processor bowl.

3 Set a strainer over a medium bowl. Place the cottage cheese in the strainer and, with the back of a wooden spoon, press through into the bowl.

4 Add the feta cheese, 2 tablespoons of the olive oil, and the cayenne pepper to the food processor bowl. With a few taps on the pulse switch, lightly mix together. Add the cottage cheese and combine everything with a few more taps.

5 Transfer the mixture to a shallow dish. Pour over the remaining olive oil and sprinkle with pepper and chives.

Octopus with Olive Oil and Vinegar

Ktopothi me Lathoxsithi

Prepare this dish a day or two before you serve it—octopus really does taste much better if left to marinate for a while. My neighbor, a fisherman, kills and prepares an octopus for me in the "old way": He bites through the nerve center that passes behind the octopus' eyes. Then he tenderizes it by throwing the octopus against a rock until he's tired. In stores, octopus is sold already cleaned and tenderized, which is just as well, because it's impossible to tenderize an octopus once it's dead. You do have to skin a store-bought octopus, but this is an easy task if you first let it cook in its own juices until the moisture has evaporated.

SERVES: 6 / Best made one or two days before serving

One 2½-pound tenderized octopus
4 tablespoons red wine vinegar ◆ 1 plump clove garlic, chopped
Coarse sea salt to taste ◆ ½ cup extra-virgin olive oil or more to taste
Small bunch of fresh thyme or flat-leaf parsley, leaves finely chopped, or
2 tablespoons dried Greek oregano, crumbled ◆ Finely cracked pepper to taste

◆

1 If it has not already been done by the fish seller, remove the eyes, mouth, and inside of the head of the octopus: cut below the eyes at the spot where the tentacles meet. Turn the pouchlike head inside out, discard the contents, and cut out and discard the eyes and mouth. Rinse the octopus well in several changes of cold water.

2 Set a heavy, nonreactive saucepan or casserole over low-medium heat. When hot, add the octopus and 2 tablespoons vinegar. Cook 5 minutes, stirring occasionally with a wooden spoon, until the octopus begins to curl (a sign that it's losing its water) and turns slightly pink. Cover the pan, reduce the heat to very low, and turn once or twice while cooking 1 hour or until

the octopus is tender; add a few tablespoons of water if necessary to prevent the octopus from sticking to the bottom of the pan. Test by inserting a thin-bladed knife into the thickest part of one tentacle.

3 Thoroughly rinse the octopus under cold water and pat dry with paper towels. Place in a bowl, cover tightly, and set aside until cold.

4 Cut the legs away from the body (head) of the octopus, then cut the body lengthwise into quarters. Peel off and discard the skin to expose the pale pink flesh (the suckers come off easily along with the skin).

Cut everything into 1½-inch pieces and place in a large bowl.

5 Place the garlic and salt to taste in a mortar or small bowl. Using a pestle or wooden spoon, pound together until well blended. Stir in the remaining 2 tablespoons vinegar, and whisk in the olive oil. Pour this sauce over the octopus pieces, tightly cover the bowl, and refrigerate until needed; turn the pieces once or twice in the marinade.

6 Place the octopus and marinade in a shallow bowl or platter. Sprinkle with thyme, parsley, or oregano, and the pepper and salt.

Marinated Fish

Psaria Marinata

*Marinated fish make a tasty and colorful meze or first course, as well as an
easy-to-serve, light lunch. I marinate fish in many different ways.
If I want to make them in a hurry, or if I am expecting guests who may not
appreciate the appearance of a whole fish (complete with head) on the
table in front of them, I use this recipe.*

SERVES: 6 for a first course, 3 as a light lunch

6 fillets (about 1½ pounds) mackerel or similar-sized firm fish
2 tablespoons red wine vinegar ◆ 1 tablespoon whole coriander seeds
2 whole cloves ◆ 4 bay leaves ◆ 1 small red onion, quartered and thinly sliced
Coarse sea salt to taste ◆ 4 tablespoons finely chopped fresh flat-leaf parsley
1 tablespoon small capers, drained ◆ Finely cracked pepper to taste
3 tablespoons extra-virgin olive oil

◆

1 Rinse the fillets and place in a nonreactive saucepan. Add the vinegar, coriander, cloves, bay leaves, and water to barely cover the fish. Slowly bring to a boil over low heat. Remove from the heat and set aside to cool.

2 Place the onion in a small bowl and cover with cold water; set aside.

3 Remove the fillets from the marinade, lay them on a board, and slice into diagonal pieces. With a spatula, carefully transfer them to a shallow serving bowl or platter. Pour the marinade through a strainer over the fish.

4 Drain the onion and squeeze dry with paper towels. In a small bowl, combine the onion, salt, and parsley. Scatter this mixture, and the capers, over the fish, and sprinkle with pepper and olive oil.

Fried Eggplant and Zucchini
Melitzanes ke Kolokithes Tiganites

In the early summer, when zucchini and eggplant are young, sweet, and crunchy, use them to make these pretty little fritters. They may be served hot, warm, or at room temperature, with bowls of olives, for a meze, or first course, or as a side dish to grilled meats.

SERVES: 8 for a first course, 4 as a side dish

3 medium zucchini ◆ 1 medium eggplant
1 teaspoon fine sea salt or to taste ◆ 6 tablespoons all-purpose flour
1 tablespoon chickpea flour (available in specialty food stores)
Olive oil for frying ◆ Juice of 1 lemon ◆ Coarse sea salt and finely cracked pepper to taste
2 tablespoons finely chopped fresh flat-leaf parsley or fresh herb of choice

◆

1 Trim off and discard the ends from the zucchini and eggplant. Cut the zucchini crosswise in half, then into ¼-inch-thick lengthwise slices. Cut the eggplant into ¼-inch-thick round slices. Layer the slices on a plate, sprinkling each layer with fine salt. Set aside for 1 hour to "sweat."

2 Combine the all-purpose flour and chickpea flour in a shallow bowl or on a plate.

3 Thoroughly dry the zucchini and eggplant slices with paper towels. Toss the slices in the flour and shake off any excess.

4 Set two large, heavy skillets or frying pans over low heat. When hot, pour in the olive oil to make a thin layer. Raise the heat slightly, and add enough slices to make a single layer in the skillets.

5 Fry until golden brown on both sides for about 8 minutes, turning once; drain on paper towels. Repeat with the remaining slices; add a few more tablespoons olive oil to the skillet if needed.

6 Arrange the slices on a warm platter, and sprinkle with lemon juice, coarse salt, pepper, and parsley (or other herb of choice).

Mama says... Combine a little chickpea flour with the all-purpose flour for fritters with an appetizingly nutty flavor.

Small Fried Fish with Garlic Sauce
Marithes Tiganites me Skordalia

*My family's favorite dishes are those that are the simplest—and the crunchiest.
Few dishes could be much simpler, or crunchier, than these little fried fish. The local
fishermen always have plenty of tiny* marithes *(whitebait),* gavros *(anchovies), and*
gopa *(bogue) among their catch, and they are often only too happy to give them
to me, for they are worth little in the market.
All sorts of fish can be prepared using this recipe, as long as they are tiny
(the whole fish is eaten, including the head) and very, very fresh. Larger fillets
of firm fish, such as mackerel or bonito, may also be used—
just cut them into bite-sized pieces and prepare them the same way.
Serve with this strong garlic sauce and plenty of lemon wedges.*

SERVES: 6

3 thick slices good-quality white bread, crusts removed, lightly toasted
½ cup water ◆ 4 to 6 plump cloves fresh garlic or to taste
½ teaspoon fine sea salt or to taste ◆ Juice of 1 small lemon ◆ Finely cracked pepper
6 to 8 tablespoons extra-virgin olive oil plus more for frying
6 tablespoons all-purpose flour ◆ 1 tablespoon chickpea flour
1 pound tiny fish such as whitebait or anchovies, washed,
cleaned, and patted dry with paper towels ◆ Lemon wedges

◆

1 Heat the oven to 130°F and warm a platter.

2 Break the bread into large chunks into a bowl,
and pour the water over. Set aside 15 minutes.

3 Place the garlic and salt in a mortar or small
bowl. Using a pestle or wooden spoon, pound

together until well blended. Transfer to a food
processor bowl.

4 To remove excess water, squeeze the bread
between paper towels, and add to the garlic with
half the lemon juice and a little pepper. With the
machine running, add the extra-virgin olive oil

in a thin steady stream until you have a thick, smooth sauce that just holds its shape; add more olive oil or water if needed to thin the mixture. Taste, add the remaining lemon juice if desired, and salt and pepper to taste. Transfer to a serving bowl, tightly cover, and set aside or refrigerate (bring back to room temperature for serving).

5 Set a large heavy sauté pan over low heat and pour in olive oil to make a ½-inch layer.

6 In a shallow bowl, combine the all-purpose flour and chickpea flour, and season with a little salt and pepper. Add the fish, toss to coat, and shake off any excess flour.

7 When the olive oil is hot, but before it reaches smoking temperature, raise the heat to low-medium and add enough fish to fill the pan without overcrowding. Fry until golden brown, turning once with a spatula (about 6 minutes).

8 As the fish become golden brown, drain on paper towels. Transfer to the warm platter and leave in the oven while you cook the rest of the fish.

9 To serve, pile the fish high on the platter and sprinkle with salt and pepper to taste. Surround with lemon wedges, and serve with garlic sauce.

Mama says...
When heating olive oil for frying, be sure to keep its temperature just below the level that causes the oil to smoke (indicated by a light haze over the surface of the oil). When olive oil reaches smoking temperature, the flavor of the dish may be spoiled and the oil's nutrients destroyed.

Cracked-Wheat Meatballs

Kephtedakia Kreas ke Pligouri

Kephtedakia are just one of the traditional dishes we serve at the communal outdoor gatherings we all enjoy so much. These highly flavored little meatballs are a big favorite with children and adults alike, for they are easy to eat and easy to make. They can be fried, baked, or grilled, and they are equally delicious warm or cold. Served with ouzo, kephtedakia are the perfect meze. They may also be served in their larger form (kephtedes) as a main course.

SERVES: 12 for a meze, 6 as a main course

1 cup cracked wheat ◆ 1 large onion, finely chopped
1 pound fresh lean lamb or beef, finely ground
2 tablespoons dried Greek oregano, crumbled ◆ 2 tablespoons red wine vinegar
Coarse sea salt and finely cracked pepper to taste
Small handful of fresh flat-leaf parsley, leaves only, finely chopped ◆ 1 large egg, beaten
Olive oil for frying ◆ 2 small red onions, quartered and thinly sliced
4 tablespoons fresh mint leaves, torn into pieces at the last minute,
or a fresh herb of choice ◆ 1 tablespoon sumac or 1 teaspoon paprika
2 tablespoons extra-virgin olive oil ◆ Lemon wedges

◆

1 Soak the cracked wheat in water to cover for 30 minutes.

2 Place the chopped onion in a small, heavy saucepan, add the water to barely cover, and slowly bring to a boil over low heat. Simmer uncovered until the water has evaporated (about 6 minutes).

3 In a large bowl, use your hand to combine the meat, cooked onion, oregano, vinegar, salt, pepper, and half the parsley. Squeeze the cracked wheat dry between paper towels and add this and the egg to the mixture. Knead together for a minute or two, until very well mixed. Tightly cover the bowl, and refrigerate 1 to 3 hours.

4 Moisten your hands with cold water and shape the meat mixture into 24 balls. Gently flatten each one into a ½-inch-thick patty (or form the mixture into 12 balls for kephtedes).

5 Set a heavy skillet or frying pan over low-medium heat and add enough olive oil to make a very thin layer. When the oil is hot (but not smoking), add one layer of meatballs. Fry, turning once, until browned on both sides (about 6 minutes); drain on paper towels. Repeat with the remainder.

6 In a medium bowl, combine the red onion, mint (or herb of choice), and remaining parsley. Spread this mixture over a platter and sprinkle with the sumac (or paprika), salt, pepper, and the extra-virgin olive oil. Arrange the kephtedakia on top. Surround with lemon wedges, and serve warm or at room temperature.

NOTE: IF PREFERRED, THE MEATBALLS MAY BE BAKED INSTEAD OF FRIED. HEAT THE OVEN TO 325°F, AND WARM A BAKING TRAY. BRUSH THE BAKING TRAY WITH OLIVE OIL AND ARRANGE THE KEPHTEDAKIA ON IT. LIGHTLY BRUSH THE KEPHTEDAKIA WITH OLIVE OIL. BAKE 25 TO 30 MINUTES, TURNING ONCE, UNTIL BROWNED ON BOTH SIDES.

Mama says...
Sumac is the pulverized berry of a piquant herb. Deep auburn in color, and with a coarse powder texture, it has a deliciously tangy, slightly acidic flavor that is perfect for bean dishes and for grilled and fried meats.

Roasted Peppers with Capers
Piperi me Kapari

Our best peppers come from the north of Greece—they are a beautiful, brilliant red, and they have a mild, almost sweet flavor. Visiting relatives bring them to me when they are in season. I grill them, stuff them, pickle them and, best of all, turn them into this little salad.

SERVES: 6 to 8

6 medium bell peppers (any color or mix of colors) ◆ 1 tablespoon red wine vinegar 5 tablespoons extra-virgin olive oil ◆ 2 tablespoons finely chopped fresh flat-leaf parsley 2 tablespoons chopped fresh fennel, dill, or chervil ◆ 2 tablespoons chopped chives or the unblemished green parts of 2 green onions, finely chopped ◆ 2 tablespoons small capers, rinsed and patted dry ◆ Coarse sea salt and finely cracked pepper to taste

1 Roast the peppers. Using tongs, hold each pepper over an open flame or place on a hot grill, turning until blistered and blackened on all sides. Transfer to a paper bag or a bowl. Close the bag or cover the bowl with plastic wrap, and set aside to cool.

2 Using your fingers, rub off and discard the skin, and discard the core and seeds (but don't rinse the peppers—water will spoil their flavor).

Slice the peppers into thin strips lengthwise and place in a bowl.

3 In a small bowl, whisk together the vinegar and olive oil. Pour the sauce over the peppers, carefully turn them to coat with the sauce, and transfer to a small serving platter.

4 Lightly chop the herbs together to mix. Sprinkle herbs, capers, salt, and pepper over the peppers.

Mama says...
For that sweet, mellow flavor of the best pepper salads, you need to first roast (or scorch) the peppers.

Fried Cheese
Saganaki

This dish is named for the two-handled frying pan (saganaki) that I, and other village cooks, use to fry the cheese. Saganaki takes only a few minutes to cook, so make it only when you are ready to eat. Bring to the table piping hot. As our cheeses are mostly generic (that is, named for their type, not for where they come from) their "character" can change with the season or their place of origin. Both kephalotyri and kasseri can sometimes be softer than is required for saganaki. If you buy your cheese in a specialty store, ask if it's suitable for frying at that moment—you might be told that another Greek cheese would be more suitable.

SERVES: 6

---

10 ounces kephalotyri or kasseri cheese ◆ 6 tablespoons all-purpose flour
Olive oil for frying ◆ Juice of ½ lemon
Finely cracked pepper ◆ 2 lemons, cut into wedges

◆

1 Heat the oven to 130°F and warm a platter.

2 Using a thin-bladed knife or cheese slicer, cut the cheese into ¼-inch slices. Cut each slice into 2-inch by 3-inch rectangles. Spread the flour on a large plate. Dredge the cheese slices and shake off any excess flour.

3 Place a heavy skillet or frying pan over low-medium heat. When hot, pour in olive oil to make a thin layer; take care not to let the oil smoke. Add enough cheese slices to the skillet to make a single layer. Fry on both sides until golden brown and crusty (about 6 minutes), turning once with a spatula. Transfer to the warm platter, and keep warm in the oven until you have fried all the slices.

4 Sprinkle the cheese with the lemon juice and pepper to taste. Serve with lemon wedges.

Tiny Stuffed Grape Leaves

Dolmadakia me Latholemono

We all have our favorite fillings for dolmadakia (the smallest, and most delicate, versions of dolmades, or stuffed grape leaves). I like to use pearl barley, currants, and plenty of fragrant herbs. These lovely little morsels are not difficult to make but they do take time, so it's worth knowing that you can prepare and freeze them before they are cooked, and they can also be made a day or two ahead of time. Serve dolmadakia warm or at room temperature.

SERVES: 12 for a meze, 6 to 8 as a first course

3 tablespoons currants ◆ 1 tablespoon red wine vinegar ◆ 5 tablespoons pearl barley
5 tablespoons extra-virgin olive oil or to taste ◆ 2 small shallots, very finely chopped
¼ teaspoon ground cinnamon ◆ 1 teaspoon dried Greek oregano, crumbled
3 tablespoons chopped blanched almonds ◆ Fine sea salt and freshly ground pepper
24 small to medium grape leaves, fresh or brine-preserved,
plus extra leaves to make 1 layer in the baking dish
2 tablespoons finely chopped fresh flat-leaf parsley or dill
Juice of ½ a small lemon ◆ Lemon wedges

◆

1 In a small bowl, combine the currants, vinegar, and 2 tablespoons water. Set aside.

2 Half fill a small saucepan with water and bring to a brisk simmer. Add the pearl barley and cook until just soft (about 15 minutes). Drain, and set aside.

3 Set a heavy saucepan over low heat and add 2 tablespoons olive oil. Add the shallots and sauté until soft (about 5 minutes). Stir in the cinnamon and oregano, then the pearl barley. Add the currants and their liquid, the almonds, and salt and pepper to taste. Cover the pan with a tight-fitting lid and remove from the heat. Set aside in a warm spot such as the back of the stove.

4 Half fill a large saucepan with water and bring to a boil. With kitchen scissors, trim off any stems from the grape leaves. First blanch the

grape leaves to be used for lining the dish: add them to the pan and simmer 3 seconds if brine-preserved, 5 seconds if fresh. Using a slotted spoon, remove the leaves and spread between paper towels to dry. Choose a heavy, flameproof dish or sauté pan, large enough to hold the dolmadakia in a single tightly packed layer, and line with these leaves, glossy sides down.

5 Blanch the remaining leaves, 5 or 6 at a time, and spread between paper towels to dry.

6 Stir the parsley or dill into the pearl barley filling, and add salt and pepper if needed.

7 Place a grape leaf on the palm of your hand, glossy side down and stem end toward your wrist. Place 1 tablespoon filling in the center of the leaf at its widest part. Pull the stem end over the filling, and fold over both sides. Firmly roll up the parcel in the direction of the leaf point.

Repeat with the remaining leaves and filling, placing each one tightly against the next one in the dish.

8 Pour 2 tablespoons olive oil and the lemon juice over the dolmadakia, and add enough water to the dish to barely reach the top of them. Arrange a plate that is slightly smaller than the dish directly on top of the dolmadakia, and place a weight (such as a large can of fruit) on the plate. Set the dish over low-medium heat and bring just to a boil. Reduce the heat to low and simmer 25 minutes. There should always be some liquid in the dish as the dolmadakia simmer; if necessary add a few tablespoons water. Remove the dish from the heat and, with the plate and weight still in place, set aside to cool.

9 Transfer the dolmadakia to a platter or to individual plates. Sprinkle with the remaining olive oil and pan juices to taste. Garnish with lemon wedges.

Mama says...
Pearl barley is one my favorite foods to use as a filling. It is an ideal choice for those of us who need to take a little care with the amount of carbohydrates we eat. Unlike rice, which quickly breaks down in our systems, it's a slow-burning carbohydrate, so it takes longer to provide us with energy.

Potato-Cheese Patties
Kephtedes Patatas

There's something about potato dishes that everyone seems to appreciate. When they are combined with herbs and cheese too, they are irresistible. As potatoes inevitably absorb some of their cooking oil, I use the finer-flavored extra-virgin olive oil to fry the kephtedes.

MAKES: 12 kephtedes or 18 kephtedakia (very small patties)

8 small boiling potatoes, skins intact, scrubbed
1 large egg, plus yolk of 1 large egg ◆ 1 tablespoon finely chopped fresh flat-leaf parsley
2 tablespoons finely chopped fresh fennel or dill (or additional fresh flat-leaf parsley)
4 green onions, including unblemished green parts, trimmed and finely chopped
Coarse sea salt and finely cracked pepper to taste
½ cup finely grated kephalotyri or feta cheese ◆ All-purpose flour for dredging
Extra-virgin olive oil for frying
A few sprigs of purslane or young arugula leaves for garnish

◆

1 Heat the oven to 375°F. Place 2 baking trays in the oven to heat.

2 Cook the potatoes in boiling water until just tender (about 12 minutes). Drain, and set aside.

3 Peel the potatoes, and pass them through a food mill fitted with the fine disk.

4 In a medium bowl, whisk together the egg and egg yolk until frothy. Add the parsley, fennel or dill, green onions, salt, and pepper. Pour this over the potatoes, add the cheese, and stir to mix. Cover the bowl and refrigerate for 30 minutes.

5 Spread the flour on a plate. Moisten your hands with cold water and pat barely dry. Shape the potato mixture into 12 balls for kephtedes or into 18 balls for kephtedakia. Flatten the balls slightly and lightly dredge with flour.

6 Brush the hot baking trays with olive oil and arrange the patties on them, 1 inch apart. Brush with olive oil. Bake 8 to 10 minutes, turn, and bake 6 to 8 minutes longer or until browned on both sides. Transfer to paper towels to drain.

7 Arrange the kephtedes on a platter, garnish with the purslane or arugula, and serve warm.

Chapter two
SOUPS

Tomato and Pasta Soup
Domatosoupa

When you have plenty of ripe tomatoes and a little good-quality chicken broth, make this lively, pretty soup. My mother likes to finish it with trachanas, a pasta made from soured sheep's milk. I prefer a sweeter, fresher flavor, so I use tiny hilopites (square-shaped pasta) and feta cheese.

SERVES: 6

¼ cup extra-virgin olive oil
8 ripe medium tomatoes, peeled and diced (juices reserved) ◆ 1 teaspoon sugar
Coarse sea salt and finely cracked pepper to taste ◆ 1 cup hot chicken broth
3 cups hot water ◆ ½ cup *hilopites* (tiny square-shaped pasta) or orzo
4 ounces barrel-aged feta cheese, or other good quality feta cheese, drained and crumbled
2 tablespoons fresh marjoram ◆ 2 tablespoons finely chopped chives

◆

1 Set a heavy saucepan over low heat.

2 When the saucepan is warm, add 3 tablespoons of the olive oil, the tomatoes and their juices, the sugar, a little salt, and a more generous quantity of pepper. Cook until the tomatoes are soft, but not disintegrating (about 5 minutes).

3 Add the broth and water, and slowly bring to a boil. Add the pasta and simmer 10 minutes or until the pasta is cooked. Check the seasonings, but remember that the feta will be salty.

4 Pour into shallow soup bowls. Sprinkle with the feta, marjoram, chives, and remaining olive oil. Serve hot or warm.

Chickpea and Spinach Soup
Revithosoupa me Spanaki

Chickpeas are a staple ingredient in my kitchen cupboard. During Lent, our longest and most serious fast, I rely on them to provide us with protein and energy. We enjoy them in a nutritious dip (see page 12), in salads, and in this warming soup.

SERVES: 6

2 cups dried chickpeas, covered by 3 inches water and soaked 6 hours or overnight ◆ 1 small onion, peeled ◆ 1 pound spinach or young beet leaves ◆ 5 tablespoons extra-virgin olive oil ◆ 1 large onion, finely chopped ◆ 1 large garlic clove, finely chopped ◆ 1 teaspoon ground coriander ◆ 2 tablespoons chopped fresh flat-leaf parsley ◆ 3 tablespoons chopped fresh fennel or dill ◆ Coarse sea salt and finely cracked pepper to taste ◆ Lemon wedges

◆

1 Drain the chickpeas and place in a large saucepan. Add water to cover by 2 inches. Bring to a boil, reduce the heat to low, and simmer 5 minutes. Drain and rinse out the saucepan. Return the chickpeas to the saucepan. Add the small onion and water to cover by at least 3 inches. Bring to a boil. Cover, reduce the heat to low, and simmer 35 to 45 minutes or until the chickpeas are soft. Drain over a bowl and reserve the cooking liquid. Discard the onion.

2 Wash (but don't dry) the spinach or beet leaves and strip the leaves from any tough stems (discard the stems). Place in a large, heavy saucepan or sauté pan, cover, and cook over low heat 2 minutes. Drain in a colander and, with a wooden spoon, press the leaves against the sides to remove as much water as possible. Coarsely chop the greens on a chopping board.

3 Set a heavy saucepan over low heat and add 3 tablespoons olive oil. Add the onion and cook until very soft, stirring occasionally (about 10 minutes). Add the garlic and coriander, cook 1 minute longer, and add the parsley, fennel or dill, spinach, salt, and pepper. Cook 1 minute.

4 Place about ¼ chickpeas and about 1 cup of their reserved cooking liquid in a food processor bowl; lightly mix. Add this to the spinach mixture with the rest of the chickpeas and their cooking liquid. Stir to mix, and add water to thin the soup to your taste. When hot, check the seasonings. Serve with a bowl of lemon wedges.

Country Bean Soup
Fassoulada

This is the great, classic soup of the Greek countryside. Delicious and sustaining, it's a good recipe to make when you are already using your oven, or it can be simmered on the stovetop. Use your best Greek olive oil here, and serve the soup with slices of cheese, olives, horta, and a good, strong wine.

SERVES: 6 to 8

2 cups dried white beans, covered by 3 inches water and soaked 6 hours or overnight

3 large ripe tomatoes, peeled and diced (juices reserved)

1 teaspoon sugar ◆ ½ cup extra-virgin olive oil ◆ 2 medium onions, finely chopped

3 medium carrots, cut into thin slices or small dice

2 stalks celery, strings removed, finely diced ◆ 1 plump clove garlic, finely chopped

2 tablespoons dried thyme or Greek oregano ◆ Small bunch of fresh flat-leaf parsley, leaves only, half finely chopped and half coarsely chopped

Finely cracked pepper to taste ◆ 8 cups water or light meat broth or a mixture

1 tablespoon tomato paste mixed with 2 tablespoons water

Coarse sea salt to taste ◆ 2 tablespoons red wine vinegar

◆

1 Drain the beans. Place in a large saucepan with water to cover by 3 inches. Bring to a boil, lower the heat, and simmer 5 minutes. Drain, rinse the beans and the saucepan, and set aside.

2 Sprinkle the tomatoes with sugar and set aside.

3 Set the clean saucepan over low-medium heat and add 4 tablespoons olive oil. Add the onions, carrots, and celery, and sauté for 15 minutes or until soft, stirring occasionally with a wooden spoon. Add the garlic, thyme or oregano, finely chopped parsley, pepper, water (or broth) and the beans. Bring slowly to a boil, cover, and simmer 1 hour or until the beans are soft but not disintegrating.

4 Add the tomatoes and their juices, tomato paste, salt, and pepper to the soup and simmer 5 minutes longer. Stir in the remaining parsley and olive oil. Sprinkle with vinegar and check the seasonings. Serve hot or warm.

Lentil Soup with Chervil
Soupa Fakes

During the spring, an especially good horta (wild green) grows on the hillsides just outside the village. It's known as chervil (kafkalithres) but, unlike our garden chervil, it has large leaves that resemble those of clover. It tastes very good in this soup. When I can't find it, I use garden chervil instead. Serve the soup with a bowl of golden-brown croutons.

SERVES: 6

1⅛ cups green or brown lentils, rinsed, and soaked 10 minutes in water to cover
3 large ripe tomatoes, peeled and finely diced (reserve juices)
1 teaspoon sugar ◆ Coarse sea salt and finely cracked pepper to taste
¼ cup extra-virgin olive oil ◆ 1 large mild onion, finely chopped
1 plump clove garlic, finely chopped ◆ 3 small potatoes, peeled and cut into small dice
1 celery stalk, strings removed, finely diced ◆ 3 bay leaves ◆ Pinch of cumin
4½ cups light chicken, meat, or vegetable broth, or water
Small handful of fresh chervil, leaves only, chopped

◆

1 Drain the lentils and place in a saucepan with water to cover. Bring to a boil, reduce the heat to low, and simmer 5 minutes. Drain.

2 Sprinkle the tomatoes with sugar, salt, and pepper.

3 Set a heavy saucepan over low heat. When warm, add the olive oil, onion, garlic, potato, and celery, and gently sauté 10 minutes, stirring occasionally. Add the bay leaves, cumin, broth

(or water), and lentils, and bring slowly to a boil. Cover, and simmer 30 minutes or until the lentils are soft. Use a slotted spoon to remove any froth that forms as it cooks. Discard the froth.

4 Add the tomatoes and their juices to the lentil mixture and gently stir to mix. Bring back to a boil and simmer 1 minute. Check the seasonings.

5 Divide the soup between warm bowls, sprinkle with chervil, and serve hot or warm.

A Pot of Vegetables and Ham

Soupa Lakhanika

We love one-pot meals in our household. They are simple to serve so they don't get in the way of our table conversation, and we can all eat as much or as little as we want. This soup is so thick and robust that you won't need to follow it with another course. Serve with slices of cheese, bowls of olives, and plenty of good bread.

SERVES: 6

8 ounces good-quality ham or bacon, cut into 3 pieces ♦ 6 bay leaves
2 sprigs of fresh or dried thyme ♦ 8 small boiling (white) onions, peeled and
quartered lengthwise ♦ 8 small carrots, peeled, left whole if tiny or cut into pieces if larger
6 small potatoes, peeled and halved or quartered ♦ 3 small turnips, peeled and quartered
3 small zucchini, trimmed and cut into 1-inch pieces ♦ 3 cups green beans, trimmed and
cut into large pieces, or 5½ cups fresh podded fava beans
5 cups white cabbage (about 6 ounces), cored and cut into thin strips
Finely cracked pepper to taste ♦ 2 plump cloves garlic, finely chopped
Coarse sea salt to taste ♦ 6 tablespoons finely chopped fresh flat-leaf parsley or mixed fresh
herbs such as marjoram, chervil, cilantro, or fennel ♦ 6 tablespoons extra-virgin olive oil

♦

1 Place the ham in a large, heavy pot. Add water to cover by 1½ inches. Add the bay leaves, thyme sprigs, onions, and carrots. Set over low heat, bring slowly to a boil, cover, and simmer 30 minutes.

2 Add the potatoes, turnips, zucchini, and beans and simmer covered 30 to 40 minutes longer or until the vegetables are cooked. Add hot water if needed to thin the soup. Add the cabbage and

simmer 5 more minutes. The ham should be soft enough to cut with a spoon, with the vegetables almost falling apart. Discard the thyme sprigs and season generously with pepper.

3 On a board, chop together the garlic, ½ teaspoon salt, and the parsley (or mixed herbs). Stir this mixture and the olive oil into the soup, and check the seasonings. Serve hot or warm.

Fisherman's Soup
Kakavia

Kakavia is so much a part of our family life that it's difficult to give a recipe for such a familiar dish. The soup base is always the same—potatoes, carrots, onions, parsley, and celery—but the fish that we use changes with the catch. My fisherman neighbor may bring me snapper, mullet, bream, or best of all, a scorpion fish. For a speedier preparation and easier eating, kakavia can be made with fish fillets (although, without the bones and heads of whole fish, the broth won't taste quite so velvety smooth). Sometimes I like to add tomatoes to the broth—instead of lemon juice— or flavor it with saffron. However you choose to make the soup, have plenty of crusty bread on the table.

SERVES: 6

2½ pounds white-fleshed fish such as snapper, bream, rockfish, monkfish, mullet, or scorpion, or 1¾ pounds fish fillets
6 tablespoons extra-virgin olive oil
12 shallots, peeled and quartered lengthwise
4 medium carrots, peeled and diagonally sliced
1 celery stalk, strings removed, very thinly sliced
Small handful of fresh flat-leaf parsley, leaves coarsely chopped
6 sprigs of lovage or celery leaves, coarsely chopped
5 small boiling potatoes, peeled and cut into pieces
Coarse sea salt and finely cracked pepper ♦ Juice of 1 small lemon
Lemon wedges

♦

1 Scale, clean, and gut the fish. If small, leave whole; if large, cut into 2 or 3 pieces.

2 Set a large, heavy saucepan or casserole over low heat and add 4 tablespoons of the olive oil. Add the shallots, carrots, and celery and cook 10 minutes, stirring occasionally, until the shallots are soft (don't let the vegetables brown). Add half the parsley, the lovage (or celery leaves), and the potatoes, and cook 1 minute longer. Cover the vegetables with water by 1 inch, raise the heat slightly, and bring to a boil. Reduce the heat to low, cover, and simmer 5 minutes.

3 Place the fish on top of the vegetables, cover the pan, and simmer 15 minutes longer or until both fish and vegetables are cooked.

4 Strain off the broth from the pan into a bowl. Carefully remove the fish from the pan onto a board; remove and discard the bones and heads. (If using fish fillets, remove and discard the skin.)

5 Return the fish to the pan and pour over the broth. Season to taste with salt and pepper. Return the pan to low heat and simmer about 5 minutes.

6 Divide the fish and vegetables between warm, shallow soup bowls and pour the broth over. Squeeze lemon juice into each bowl and sprinkle with the remaining olive oil and parsley. Serve with lemon wedges.

Mama says...
Lovage grows wild in the rocky ravines near our coast. Its dark green leaves are an essential part of our kakavia. It's easy to grow in the garden, as is the celery we grow for its leaves. Throughout the spring, you may find large bundles of this kind of celery, which has short thin stems and flavorful dark green leaves (unlike stick celery, with its very pale green, slightly bitter leaves), in specialty produce stores.

Chicken and Rice Soup

Soupa Avgolemono

Chicken soup is always a great pick-me-up. It's even better when made with eggs and lemon juice, as it is in our village.

SERVES: 6

5 cups good-quality chicken broth or broth and water
¼ cup short-grain white rice ♦ 3 large organic eggs, separated
Juice of 2 small lemons, strained ♦ Sea salt and finely cracked pepper
2 tablespoons finely chopped fresh flat-leaf parsley

♦

1 Set a large, heavy saucepan over low-medium heat, add the broth (or broth and water), and bring to a boil. Add the rice, reduce the heat to low, and simmer 15 minutes or until the rice is cooked.

2 Just before you are ready to serve the soup, place the egg whites in a large bowl. With a wire whisk or electric mixer, whisk until thick but not stiff. Whisk in the egg yolks. Still whisking, slowly add the lemon juice and whisk 1 minute longer. Remove a ladleful of the hot soup from the pan and, holding it about 12 inches above the bowl, slowly pour it into the egg mixture. Make sure you whisk constantly.

3 Remove the soup from the heat and whisk in the egg mixture. Return the pan to a very low heat. Continue to carefully stir the soup until barely hot; don't let it boil or it will curdle, and take care not to break up the rice. Add salt and pepper to taste, and divide between warm bowls or transfer to a warm soup tureen. Sprinkle with parsley and serve immediately.

Chapter three
MAIN COURSES

Baked Fish Plaki

Psaria Plaki

*We Peloponnese cooks are famous throughout Greece for our plaki, or layered,
baked dishes. Their fine flavor comes from our wonderful olive oil, which we have in
abundance, and our love of slow baking. John Dory, mullet, and bream are my
favorite fish to use in this recipe, but almost any firm-fleshed fish
can be baked this way.*

SERVES: 6

2 firm-fleshed fish such as mullet or bream, about 1¼ pounds each
Coarse sea salt and finely cracked pepper to taste ◆ Juice of 1 small lemon
½ cup extra-virgin olive oil ◆ 3 tablespoons dried Greek oregano
3 plump cloves garlic, each one cut lengthwise into 2 or 3 pieces
2 small to medium onions, quartered and very thinly sliced
6 large ripe tomatoes, peeled; dice 4, and thinly slice 2 (keep separate)
1 teaspoon sugar ◆ Small bunch of fresh flat-leaf parsley, leaves finely chopped
5 medium boiling potatoes, scrubbed or peeled and thinly sliced
4 bay leaves, each one broken in half ◆ 1 cup dry white wine ◆ Lemon wedges

◆

1 Rinse the fish and dry with paper towels.
With a small, sharp knife, cut 2 deep, parallel
incisions on both sides of each one. Rub the fish
inside and out with salt and pepper, half the
lemon juice, and 1 tablespoon olive oil. Sprinkle
half the oregano inside the fish cavities, and
divide the garlic between them.

2 Cover the prepared fish and refrigerate
30 minutes to 1 hour.

3 Heat the oven to 350°F.

4 Place a large, heavy skillet or frying pan over
low heat and add 3 tablespoons of the olive oil.
Add the onions, and sauté until soft (about
6 minutes). Add the diced tomatoes, the sugar,
and half the parsley. Season with salt and pepper
and simmer 10 minutes; set aside.

5 Brush a heavy baking dish with 2 tablespoons olive oil. Dry the potato slices with paper towels, and arrange in the dish. Sprinkle with the remaining lemon juice and oregano. Pour half the tomato sauce over and scatter with bay leaves.

6 Lay the fish on top and cover with the sliced tomatoes. Pour over the remaining tomato sauce and olive oil, and the white wine. Season generously with salt and pepper.

7 Cover the dish with aluminum foil and bake 30 minutes. Reduce the oven temperature to 325°F and bake uncovered 15 to 20 minutes longer or until the fish is cooked. (To check, insert a thin-bladed knife into the thickest part of the fish and ease open the flakes—they should be the same color all through.)

8 Sprinkle with the rest of the parsley and serve from the dish, with lemon wedges.

Fish with Herbs
Psaria ke Votana

During the late spring and early fall we have plenty of fish in our waters. Sometimes, I like to marinate them, and flavor them with plenty of herbs—in our house, we all like those strong flavors. This marinade works well with whole fish or with fish fillets, which are much easier to prepare. Serve with potatoes and horta.

SERVES: 6

**Six fish fillets, 4 to 5 ounces each or six whole fish such as mullet or small bream, 7 to 8 ounces each, gutted and cleaned
Coarse sea salt and finely cracked pepper to taste ◆ 2 tablespoons white wine vinegar
½ cup dry white wine ◆ 2 teaspoons whole coriander seeds
6 peppercorns ◆ 2 plump cloves garlic, peeled and bruised ◆ 10 bay leaves
Olive oil for frying ◆ All-purpose flour for dredging
1 teaspoon dried Greek oregano, crumbled
2 tablespoons finely chopped fresh flat-leaf parsley or cilantro**

◆

1 Sprinkle the fish with a little salt and, more generously, with pepper. Place in a bowl, cover, and refrigerate for 15 minutes.

2 In a small, nonreactive saucepan, combine the vinegar, wine, coriander seeds, peppercorns, garlic, and 4 bay leaves. Bring to a boil, and reduce the heat to low. Simmer uncovered for 15 minutes; set aside.

3 Set a heavy skillet or sauté pan over low heat and pour in olive oil to make a thin layer.

Dredge the fish with flour and shake off any excess. When the oil is hot, but not smoking, fry the fish until golden brown on both sides (about 6 minutes); turn once with a spatula. Drain on paper towels.

4 Transfer the fish to a shallow serving bowl. Sprinkle with the remaining bay leaves, and pour the wine over through a strainer (discard the flavorings). Sprinkle with oregano and parsley or cilantro, and serve warm or at room temperature.

Swordfish with Tomato Sauce and Olives
Xiphias me Saltsa Domatas

Use swordfish steaks, or other firm-fleshed fish fillets or steaks, for this colorful, easily prepared dish, which may be served hot or at room temperature. Fried Eggplant and Zucchini (see page 19) or Slow-Baked Zucchini (see page 83) are both good choices for side dishes. Retsina, our resin-flavored wine, is the perfect drink to serve.

SERVES: 6

Three large (about 8 ounces each) or six smaller (about 5 ounces each) swordfish fillets, or fillets of other firm-fleshed fish such as tuna or bass
Juice of 1 small lemon ◆ Coarse sea salt and finely cracked pepper to taste
½ cup extra-virgin olive oil ◆ 1 medium onion, finely chopped
1 plump clove garlic, finely chopped ◆ 1 tablespoon ground coriander
8 large ripe tomatoes, peeled and diced (juices reserved) ◆ 1 teaspoon honey
One 3-inch cinnamon stick, broken in half or ½ teaspoon ground cinnamon
2 small sprigs of fresh or dried rosemary
4 tablespoons finely chopped fresh flat-leaf parsley ◆ ⅓ cup dry white wine
12 Greek olives such as Amfissa, Thasos, or Atalanti, rinsed, pitted, and halved

◆

1 Heat the oven to 350°F.

2 Rub the fillets on both sides with lemon juice, salt, and pepper. Place in a shallow dish and pour over 3 tablespoons of the olive oil. Cover and refrigerate 30 minutes.

3 Set a large, heavy sauté pan over low heat and add 3 tablespoons of the olive oil. Add the onion and cook until soft (about 6 minutes); stir occasionally. Add the garlic and coriander and cook 1 minute longer. Add the tomatoes and their juices, the honey, cinnamon, rosemary sprigs, and half the parsley. Raise the heat to low-medium and simmer 15 minutes or until the sauce remains separated for a few seconds when you draw a wooden spoon across the bottom of the pan; discard the rosemary sprigs. Add the wine, and season with a little salt and pepper.

4 Set a heavy skillet or sauté pan over low-medium heat and add the remaining olive oil. When hot, but not smoking, sauté the fillets on both sides until pale golden brown, about 6 minutes; carefully turn once with a spatula.

5 Transfer the fish to a heavy baking dish and pour over the sauce and any olive oil remaining in the skillet. Cover and bake 30 minutes.

6 Spread the olives over the fish and bake uncovered for 5 minutes or until the fish is cooked. (To check, insert a thin-bladed knife into one fillet and gently ease open—it should be the same color all through.) Add salt and pepper if necessary.

7 Either serve from the baking dish or transfer to a platter, then sprinkle with remaining parsley.

◆

Fried Squid with Mayonnaise
Kalamaria Tiganita me Mayonaiza

This is a dish that doesn't wait for guests—the squid should be fried when everyone is at the table. Squid cook quickly but become tough if cooked too long or left to cool.

SERVES: 6

MAYONNAISE
Yolks of 2 eggs, at room temperature ◆ ½ teaspoon Dijon mustard
½ cup extra-virgin olive oil ◆ 2 tablespoons freshly squeezed lemon juice or to taste
1 tablespoon capers, drained and coarsely chopped
3 tablespoons chopped chervil or 2 tablespoons finely chopped fresh flat-leaf parsley
Fine sea salt and finely cracked pepper

SQUID
1½ pounds squid, cleaned, with body and tentacles separated ◆ ¾ cup all-purpose flour
2 tablespoons chickpea flour ◆ ½ tablespoon dried Greek oregano, crumbled
Fine sea salt and finely cracked pepper ◆ Olive oil for frying ◆ 2 lemons cut into wedges

1 In a shallow bowl or dish, whisk together the egg yolks and mustard. Add half the extra-virgin olive oil, drop by drop, whisking constantly, and pausing once or twice to add a few drops of lemon juice. Slowly add the remaining oil in a thin stream, whisking all the time. Stir in the capers and chervil (or parsley). Add salt and pepper. Transfer to a serving dish, cover, and set aside.

2 Using a sharp knife, cut the squid bodies into ½-inch-wide rings and cut the tentacles into ½-inch-long pieces.

3 In a shallow bowl, combine the all-purpose flour, chickpea flour, oregano, salt, and pepper.

Add the squid pieces and toss to coat; shake off any excess flour.

4 Set a heavy skillet or sauté pan over low heat and add olive oil to make a ½-inch layer (or use a deep-fat fryer). Heat to very hot (but not smoking temperature).

5 Fry the squid until golden brown and crisp on the outside, but still moist within (about 2 minutes); turn once if necessary. Drain on paper towels.

6 Transfer to a warm serving platter. Serve with bowls of lemon wedges and mayonnaise.

NOTE: MAYONNAISE MAY BE STORED FOR UP TO 6 HOURS: STIR 1 TABLESPOON BOILING WATER INTO THE MAYONNAISE, TIGHTLY COVER THE BOWL, AND REFRIGERATE.

◆

Mama says...
If your mayonnaise curdles, don't worry. Place one egg yolk in a clean bowl and slowly add the curdled mayonnaise, whisking constantly.

Roast Quail in Grape Leaves
Ortika sto Fourno

Grape leaves make the ideal lid, or cover, for our roasted dishes. They are biodegradable, grow freely, and also impart a delicate flavor to the dish during baking. Quail have very little fat, and wild quail, which are the ones I use, are very lean. We usually spit-roast them, but they are also very good oven-roasted. Serve with orzo or Macaroni with Herbs and Cheese (see page 103).

SERVES: 6

16 large grape leaves, fresh or brine-preserved, or enough to make 2 layers in the baking dish ◆ 6 quail, ready for the oven ◆ 6 tablespoons extra-virgin olive oil
6 sprigs of dried Greek oregano or thyme ◆ Juice of 1 lemon
Coarse sea salt and finely cracked pepper to taste
½ cup light chicken broth or water ◆ Lemon wedges

◆

1 Heat the oven to 350°F.

2 Half fill a large saucepan with water and bring to a boil. Trim off any stems from the grape leaves. Add the leaves to the pan and simmer 3 seconds if brine-preserved, 5 seconds if fresh; remove with a slotted spoon and spread on paper towels to dry.

3 Line an ample roasting pan or baking dish with half the leaves, glossy sides down.

4 Rub the quail with 3 tablespoons of the olive oil and place a sprig of oregano (or thyme) inside the cavity of each one; arrange in the roasting pan. Sprinkle with half the lemon juice, salt, and pepper and cover the quail with the remaining grape leaves. Pour over the remaining olive oil, and add the broth (or water) to the pan. Bake 35 to 45 minutes or until the quail are tender and lightly browned; baste once or twice (raising the leaves as you do this), and remove the leaves for the last 5 minutes of baking time if necessary.

5 Discard the top grape leaves. Transfer the quail to a warm platter and add salt and pepper to taste. Add the remaining lemon juice to the pan juices and gently shake the pan to mix together. Place the pan on a low heat to warm. Pour into a warm bowl or sauceboat and serve with the quail.

Chicken and Potatoes in the Oven
Kotopoulo ke Patates sto Fourno

Rigani, our favorite herb, grows in wild abundance on the hillsides surrounding our village. It's a particularly pungent variety of oregano, and we consider it to have great health benefits. In our kitchens, we always use rigani dried, not fresh. Look for it in Greek, and other good specialty markets.

SERVES: 6

Juice of 1 large lemon ◆ **1 tablespoon Dijon mustard** ◆ **1 teaspoon honey**
6 tablespoons extra-virgin olive oil
One 4-pound chicken, cut into 6 serving pieces or 6 large chicken pieces
(about 3½ pounds), excess fat and skin discarded, if desired
1½ pounds roasting potatoes, cut lengthwise into large pieces
Coarse sea salt and finely cracked pepper to taste ◆ **4 plump cloves garlic, peeled**
3 tablespoons dried Greek oregano ◆ **1 cup chicken broth or water**
4 tablespoons finely chopped fresh flat-leaf parsley

◆

1 Heat the oven to 375°F.

2 In a small bowl, combine half the lemon juice with the mustard, honey, and 2 tablespoons olive oil. By hand, rub this mixture over the chicken pieces and arrange in a single layer in a heavy roasting pan or baking dish.

3 Arrange the potatoes between the chicken pieces. Sprinkle with salt and pepper, and push the garlic cloves in among the potatoes. Pour the remaining olive oil over, and sprinkle with half the oregano. Pour the broth (or water) into the dish. Bake uncovered for 15 minutes.

4 Pour the remaining lemon juice over the potatoes. Reduce the oven temperature to 350°F. Bake 40 minutes longer or until the chicken is cooked and the potatoes are browned; baste 2 or 3 times.

5 Serve from the dish or transfer the chicken, potatoes, and garlic to a warm platter. Sprinkle with the remaining oregano and the parsley.

Lamb Chops with Eggplants
Arni me Melitzanes

I love the combination of flavors here. To make this dish, you will need two large skillets and a good sense of timing. (If this seems daunting, you may cook the eggplants ahead of time.) Serve with orzo.

SERVES: 6

12 tiny (about 3 ounces each) lamb chops or 6 medium (about 5 ounces each) lamb chops
10 tablespoons extra-virgin olive oil ◆ Coarse sea salt and finely cracked pepper to taste
18 baby eggplants, about 2 inches long, or 3 large eggplants
1 anchovy fillet, rinsed and patted dry ◆ 1 tablespoon capers, rinsed and patted dry
4 tablespoons chopped fresh flat-leaf parsley ◆ 1 tablespoon dried Greek oregano
8 Greek olives such as Amfissa or Thasos, pitted and coarsely chopped
Juice of 1 large lemon ◆ 4 tablespoons chopped chives

◆

1 Trim off any fat from the lamb chops. With your hand, rub the chops with 3 tablespoons of the olive oil, and sprinkle with salt and pepper. Place in a bowl, cover, and refrigerate.

2 Slice off the eggplant stem ends. With the point of a small paring knife, make 2 or 3 short incisions in each baby eggplant. Or cut the large eggplants into 1½-inch dice.

3 Set a heavy skillet or sauté pan over low-medium heat and add 4 tablespoons of the olive oil. When hot, add the eggplants and sauté on all sides until the skins are a little shriveled and browned (about 10 minutes); use a spatula to move them around the skillet. Shaking the skillet occasionally, reduce the heat to low and continue to cook for 10 minutes longer or until the eggplants are soft. (Or sauté the diced eggplants on all sides until well browned, about 15 minutes.) Pat with paper towels.

4 While the eggplants are cooking, set a second skillet or frying pan, large enough to hold the chops in a single layer, over low-medium heat. When hot, add the chops and their marinade. Sauté until well browned (or to taste) on both sides, turning once (about 8 minutes).

5 Combine the anchovy, capers, parsley, oregano, and olives on a cutting board; with a large knife, chop everything together.

6 Arrange the chops on one side of a warm platter and the eggplants on the other side. Return the skillet you used to cook the chops back onto low heat. Add the lemon juice and, with a wooden spoon, stir in the browned bits from the sides and bottom of the skillet. Add the remaining olive oil, heat to very warm, and pour over the chops. Spread the olive mixture over the eggplants, and sprinkle the chives over the chops. Serve hot or warm.

◆

Lamb and Artichoke Lathera
Arni ke Aginares Lathera

Many different vegetables can be used for this dish, but I especially like artichokes. Their season coincides with the time of the year when lamb tastes best—early spring. On other occasions, try very young fava beans in their pods, whole green beans, eggplants, or tiny zucchini. For the best flavor, use lamb on the bone.

SERVES: 6

10 tablespoons extra-virgin olive oil or to taste
2½ pounds tiny lamb chops or other cut of lamb on the bone or 1½ pounds boneless lamb, such as neck fillet, trimmed and cut into large bite-sized pieces
2 medium onions, quartered and thinly sliced ◆ 1 clove garlic, finely chopped
1 teaspoon ground coriander ◆ 3 medium tomatoes, peeled and diced (reserve juices)
1 teaspoon honey or sugar ◆ 1 tablespoon tomato paste mixed with 2 tablespoons water
1 tablespoon dried Greek oregano ◆ 4 tablespoons finely chopped fresh flat-leaf parsley
1 cup dry white wine or water ◆ Coarse sea salt and finely cracked pepper to taste
6 fresh artichoke hearts, quartered

1 Place a large, heavy saucepan or casserole over low-medium heat and add 3 tablespoons of the olive oil. Add the lamb and sauté until lightly browned on all sides (about 8 minutes); with a slotted spoon, transfer to a plate and set aside.

2 Reduce the heat to low, and add 2 tablespoons olive oil to the pan. Add the onions and cook, stirring occasionally, until soft (about 10 minutes). Add the garlic and coriander, and heat until their aromas rise, about 1 minute. Add the tomatoes and their juices, honey, tomato paste, oregano, and half the parsley, and simmer uncovered for 10 minutes.

3 Return the meat to the pan. Add the wine, salt, and pepper. Bring to a boil, tightly cover the pan, reduce the heat to low, and simmer 30 minutes.

4 Meanwhile, half fill a large saucepan with water, bring to a boil, and cook the artichoke hearts over medium heat for 5 minutes; drain.

5 Add the artichokes to the meat with the remaining olive oil. Cover, and continue cooking over low heat 20 minutes longer or until the artichokes are very tender. Check the seasonings.

6 Transfer the meat, artichokes, and sauce to a shallow serving dish. Sprinkle with the remaining parsley, and serve hot or warm.

Mama says...
When I pick the first spiky, pearl-green artichokes in my garden each spring, I know that another winter is finally behind me. My grandmother always insisted that we eat plenty of artichokes—she said that they "gave new life to old bones." In fact, I now understand what this old saying means—these lovely vegetables play a part in invigorating a sluggish circulation after all those heavy winter foods.

Moussaka

Moussakas

Moussakas does take time and care to prepare properly, but there's no substitute for its wonderful appearance and homey flavor. I like to make it with a mixture of vegetables, unlike the more common recipe made only with eggplants. Like so many of our great dishes, this is one that will feed that unexpected guest, and it can be made ahead of time and reheated. A small tapsi (a round baking pan) is the perfect dish to use for moussakas, but any deep baking dish is suitable.

SERVES: 8 to 10

MEAT SAUCE

5 tablespoons extra-virgin olive oil ◆ 2 large onions, finely chopped
1 celery stalk, strings removed, very finely chopped
2 pounds lean lamb or beef, or a mixture, finely minced
1 cup dry red wine ◆ 5 large tomatoes, peeled and diced (juices reserved)
1 teaspoon sugar ◆ 1 tablespoon tomato paste mixed with 2 tablespoons water
Small bunch of fresh flat-leaf parsley, leaves finely chopped
½ cup meat broth or water ◆ 3 tablespoons dried Greek oregano
1 tablespoon ground cinnamon ◆ 1 teaspoon grated nutmeg
Fine sea salt and finely cracked pepper to taste ◆ 2 large eggplants (about 1 pound)
2 medium zucchini ◆ 5 tablespoons extra-virgin olive oil or more if needed
2 medium boiling potatoes, scrubbed or peeled, cut into large pieces, and boiled 5 minutes

WHITE SAUCE

4 tablespoons unsalted butter ◆ 4 tablespoons all-purpose flour
2 cups milk, heated to very warm
¾ cup cottage cheese, drained and pressed through a strainer
⅓ cup feta cheese, drained and finely grated
6 large eggs ◆ ½ cup grated graviera, kephalotyri, or parmesan cheese

1 Heat the oven to 350°F.

2 Make the meat sauce. Set a large, heavy skillet or sauté pan over low heat and add the olive oil. When warm, add the onion and celery and sauté until soft, about 6 minutes. Raise the heat to low-medium, add the meat, and sauté until lightly browned, about 10 minutes. Break up any lumps with a wooden spoon, and stir occasionally.

3 Add the wine, and boil until evaporated, about 3 minutes. Add the tomatoes and their juices, the sugar, and the tomato paste. Reduce the heat to low, and simmer 10 minutes. Stir in the parsley, broth (or water), oregano, cinnamon, nutmeg, salt, and pepper. Simmer uncovered for 40 minutes or until almost all the liquid has evaporated. Check the seasonings (the sauce should be highly flavored). Remove from the heat and set aside for 10 minutes. Cover and set aside (or refrigerate for up to 24 hours).

4 Prepare the vegetables. Trim off both ends of the eggplants and zucchini. Cut the eggplants into ¼-inch-thick crosswise slices and the zucchini into ¼-inch-thick lengthwise slices; cut these crosswise in half. Cut the potatoes into ¼-inch-thick slices.

5 Set a large, heavy skillet or frying pan over low-medium heat and add 3 tablespoons of the olive oil. When hot, place a single layer of the eggplant slices in the pan. Fry until dark golden brown on both sides, turning once, about 5 minutes. Drain on paper towels. Repeat with the remaining eggplant and zucchini slices, adding oil to the skillet each time you add more slices.

6 Make the white sauce. Melt the butter in a medium, heavy saucepan over low heat. When melted, add the flour, and stir with a wooden spoon for 1 minute, until smooth. Add the milk, about ¼ cup at a time, stirring constantly. Bring to a boil, still stirring, and remove the pan from the heat; set aside 10 minutes to cool slightly. Then combine the cottage cheese and feta cheese and stir into the white sauce.

7 In a bowl, beat the eggs until pale and frothy with a whisk or electric mixer. Add ⅓ sauce and stir until smooth. Add the remaining mixture and combine. Add salt and pepper. Set aside.

8 Layer the potato slices over the bottom of a large 3- to 4-inch-deep baking dish, cover with ⅓ meat sauce, and pour over 4 tablespoons of the white sauce. Layer ⅔ of the zucchini slices on top (or a mixture of zucchini and eggplant), cover with another ⅓ of the meat sauce, then a little more white sauce. Layer the rest of the zucchini, and ⅓ of the eggplant on top, and cover with the remaining meat sauce. Make a final layer with the remaining eggplant slices, cover with the remaining white sauce, and sprinkle with graviera cheese.

9 Bake uncovered for 1 hour. If the top appears to be browning too quickly, loosely cover with aluminum foil. Don't press down, or the crust will come off with the foil. Serve hot or warm.

Pan-Fried Lamb's Liver

Sikotakia Tiganita

This is a quick dish to make, and a good choice for those days when you want something very tasty in a hurry.

SERVES: 4 to 6

1 pound lamb's liver ◆ All-purpose flour for dredging
6 tablespoons extra-virgin olive oil or more to taste
Coarse sea salt and finely cracked pepper to taste ◆ 3 tablespoons red wine vinegar
Small bunch of fresh flat-leaf parsley, leaves coarsely chopped
2 tablespoons small capers, drained
1 small red onion, quartered and thinly sliced

◆

1 Trim off any membranes and cut the liver into thin slices. Lightly dredge with flour, shaking off the excess.

2 Set a large, heavy skillet or frying pan over low-medium heat and add 4 tablespoons of the olive oil. When hot, add enough liver slices to make a single layer; fry until brown and a little crusty on both sides, about 5 minutes. Sprinkle generously with salt and pepper. Add the vinegar to the skillet, reduce the heat to low, and cook 1 minute longer. Shake the skillet once or twice to distribute the sauce.

3 Transfer the liver to a warm platter. Stir in all the browned bits from the sides and bottom of the skillet, and add the remaining olive oil. Warm through, and pour this sauce over the liver. Sprinkle with the parsley, capers, and onion. Serve hot or warm.

Veal Pot Roast

Pastitsada

We prefer the milder flavor of veal to that of older beef, especially in simple pot roasts such as this one. Although every village cook has a favorite way to make pastitsada, we all agree on one thing—it's always served with pasta and grated cheese.

SERVES: 6

2½ pounds top round veal or beef ◆ 1 teaspoon allspice
Finely cracked pepper and coarse sea salt to taste ◆ 5 tablespoons extra-virgin olive oil
2 medium onions, finely chopped ◆ 3 plump cloves garlic, crushed or finely chopped
6 ripe, medium tomatoes, peeled and diced (reserve juices) ◆ 6 cloves ◆ 6 bay leaves
1 cinnamon stick, broken into 3 pieces ◆ 1 tablespoon tomato paste mixed with
2 tablespoons water ◆ ½ cup dry red wine ◆ 2 tablespoons capers, rinsed and patted dry
4 tablespoons finely chopped fresh flat-leaf parsley ◆ 1 tablespoon dried Greek oregano

◆

1 Heat the oven to 350°F.

2 Cut the meat into 12 pieces, place in a bowl, and sprinkle with allspice, salt, and pepper.

3 Set a large, heavy casserole or saucepan over low-medium heat and add the olive oil. Add the meat, and sauté on all sides until lightly browned, about 8 minutes. Transfer to a bowl with a slotted spoon.

4 Add the onions to the casserole, reduce the heat to low, and sauté 5 minutes, stirring occasionally. Add the garlic and cook 1 minute longer. Add the tomatoes, cloves, bay leaves, cinnamon stick pieces, tomato paste, and wine. Raise the heat slightly and bring to a boil.

5 Return the meat to the casserole, gently stir, and bring back to a boil. Cover and bake 1½ hours or until the meat is tender. If the pan juices are still watery after 1¼ hours, bake uncovered for the last 15 minutes. Check the seasonings.

6 Chop together the capers and parsley to mix.

7 Transfer the meat and sauce to a warm platter, and spread the parsley mixture and oregano over. Serve with Macaroni with Herbs and Cheese (see page 103).

Beef and Okra
Moschari me Bamies

Okra has only a short season, so when it's ready to gather in my garden, I prepare it as often as I can. I love its rather strange, slightly acidic flavor, but it can be tricky to cook—if the pods burst in cooking, the sauce turns gelatinous. To prevent this, and to keep the slender pods deliciously juicy, I first salt them, to shrivel them a little, and add them to the dish toward the end of the cooking time.

SERVES: 6

1½ pounds fresh okra, trimmed ◆ Juice of 2 small lemons ◆ 1 tablespoon coarse sea salt
½ cup extra-virgin olive oil ◆ 2 pounds lean beef, preferably rump or other good braising cut
2 medium onions, thinly sliced ◆ 1 clove garlic, finely chopped
Large pinch of ground cloves ◆ ½ tablespoon ground cumin
6 ripe tomatoes, peeled and diced (reserve juices) ◆ 1 teaspoon honey
1 tablespoon dried thyme, crumbled ◆ ½ cup meat broth or dry white wine or water
Finely cracked pepper to taste
Small bunch of fresh flat-leaf parsley, leaves coarsely chopped

◆

1 Spread the okra in a single layer on a baking tray. Sprinkle with the juice of 1 lemon and half the salt, and set aside 1 hour.

2 Heat the oven to 375°F.

3 Set a large, heavy sauté pan or skillet over low-medium heat and add 3 tablespoons of the olive oil. Add the meat, and sauté until lightly browned on all sides, about 8 minutes. Cook in two batches if necessary, and add a little more

olive oil each time. Transfer to a heavy casserole or baking dish.

4 Add the onion to the pan, reduce the heat to low, and sauté 10 minutes or until soft. Stir in the garlic and cook until aromatic, about 1 minute. Add the cloves, cumin, tomatoes and their juices, and the honey. Raise the heat to low-medium, bring to a boil, and simmer 5 minutes. Add the thyme, broth or wine (or water), ½ cup water, a little salt, and a generous amount of

pepper, and pour this sauce over the meat. Cover the casserole and bake 1 hour or until the meat is cooked.

5 Meanwhile, rinse the okra, and carefully pat dry with paper towels. Set a large, heavy sauté pan or skillet over low heat and add 3 tablespoons olive oil. Add the okra and sauté, rolling the pods gently around the pan with a wooden spoon until they begin to change color, about 6 minutes. Drain on paper towels.

6 Add the okra to the casserole and cover again. Carefully shake the casserole to combine everything (stirring may damage the okra).

7 Uncover, return the casserole to the oven, and bake 15 minutes longer.

8 Sprinkle with the remaining lemon juice and olive oil and, very gently, shake the casserole. Check the seasonings, sprinkle the parsley over, and serve from the casserole.

◆

Beef Stew with Small Onions
Stifado

Stifado is the name we give to any dish that contains an equal quantity of small onions to meat (or octopus or snails). In the fall, rabbit and hare are our favorite meats to prepare this way. But I like beef too, especially shin of veal (in Greece, year-old beef), which produces a sauce with a soft, rich texture.

SERVES: 6

1½ pounds small boiling onions or shallots ◆ 7 tablespoons extra-virgin olive oil
2 pounds shin of veal, cut into serving slices by the butcher, or 1½ pounds top round of beef or veal rump ◆ ½ tablespoon allspice ◆ 1 teaspoon finely cracked pepper
1½ tablespoons ground coriander ◆ 3 tablespoons dried marjoram ◆ ¼ cup red wine vinegar
Peel (orange part only) of ½ organic orange, removed in strips ◆ 1 tablespoon honey
1 cinnamon stick, broken into large pieces ◆ 8 bay leaves
1½ pounds ripe tomatoes, peeled and diced (reserve juices)
Coarse sea salt to taste ◆ 4 tablespoons chopped fresh flat-leaf parsley

1 Heat the oven to 350°F.

2 Half fill a large saucepan with water and bring to a boil. With a small knife, trim each end from the onions and rub off as much of the brown outer skins as possible. Cook in boiling water for 5 minutes and drain. When cool enough to handle, peel the onions.

3 Place a heavy casserole over low-medium heat and add 3 tablespoons olive oil. When hot, add the onions and sauté 10 minutes. Transfer to a bowl.

4 Meanwhile, thoroughly rinse the shin of veal to remove any tiny bone splinters. Pat dry with paper towels. Or trim any fat from the stewing meat, and cut into 2-inch cubes.

5 Add 2 tablespoons olive oil to the casserole, raise the heat to medium, and add half the meat. Sauté on all sides until lightly browned, about 6 minutes. Transfer to the bowl. Add another 2 tablespoons olive oil to the casserole and repeat with the remaining meat. Sprinkle with allspice, pepper, coriander, and marjoram. Add the vinegar, and scrape in any browned bits from the sides of the casserole. Let it bubble for a few minutes, then add the orange peel, honey, cinnamon stick, bay leaves, tomatoes and their juices, and salt; stir to mix. Return the meat and onions to the casserole. Cover tightly, and bake 1½ hours or until the meat is very tender and the sauce has thickened. Check the seasonings.

6 Transfer to a serving bowl and sprinkle with parsley.

Mama says...

I keep a tall, round clay pot, or pithoi, in a sheltered corner of my courtyard. It contains my vinegar supply. Here, in the village, we only use vinegar made from wine. Whenever I need vinegar for cooking or for the table, I just dip a wooden ladle into the pot and take out what I need. Every week or so, I pour a bottle of wine into the pithoi, so I always have plenty of vinegar. We all love its appetizingly tangy taste, and I'm sure it keeps my family in good health.

Chicken Fricassée

Kotopoulo Fricassée

This is one of our great classic stews. Light and lemony, it's the perfect dish for a sunny spring day, especially when accompanied by a bottle or two of new-season retsina. This version calls for chicken, but lamb is often used also. I prefer to use young wild greens rather than lettuce, but lettuce is easier to find in grocery stores. There's plenty of delicious sauce, so have bread on the table, as well as boiled or steamed young potatoes and carrots.

SERVES: 6

3 whole chicken breasts, with bones, skin, and fat discarded
5 tablespoons extra-virgin olive oil ◆ 1 celery stalk, strings removed, finely diced
12 green onions, including unblemished green parts, trimmed and thinly sliced
2 heads of endive or romaine lettuce, outer leaves and
tough stems discarded, and thinly sliced (ribbons)
Bunch of fresh dill, chopped ◆ Coarse sea salt and finely cracked pepper to taste
2 cups chicken broth or water ◆ Strained juice of 2 small lemons
2 eggs, separated

◆

1 Sever each chicken breast to make 6 half-breasts, then cut each half-breast crosswise into 2 or 3 diagonal pieces.

2 Set a large, heavy saucepan or casserole over low-medium heat and add the olive oil. When hot, add the chicken and sauté until lightly browned on both sides, about 6 minutes.

3 Reduce the heat to low and add the celery, green onions, lettuce, and half the dill. Stir with a wooden spoon until the lettuce wilts, about 2 minutes. Season with salt and pepper. Add the chicken broth. Raise the heat to low-medium and bring slowly to a boil. Cover the pan, reduce the heat to low, and simmer 40 minutes or until the chicken is cooked. Remove the pan from the heat.

4 Add half the lemon juice and, holding the cover firmly in place, shake the pan to evenly distribute the juice.

5 In a large bowl, whisk the egg whites with a wire whisk or electric mixer until they hold soft peaks. Add the yolks, and whisk 1 minute longer. Remove 1 ladleful of cooking liquid from the pan and slowly pour into the egg mixture, whisking all the time.

6 Pour this sauce into the pan as you stir with a wooden spoon. Return the pan to very low heat and, stirring constantly, cook until the sauce is creamy, about 2 minutes; don't let the sauce boil.

7 Immediately remove the pan from the heat and transfer the contents to a warm, shallow bowl or serving dish. Check the seasonings, and sprinkle with the rest of the lemon juice. Garnish with the remaining dill and serve immediately.

◆

Shrimps in a Pot
Garithes Saganaki

This simple one-pot meal is cooked first on the stovetop, then in the oven for the last 10 minutes. To make life easier for you, it can be prepared ahead of time and baked just before serving. For an especially attractive table, present the shrimps in individual pots. Like so much good home-cooked food, garithes saganaki is now a favorite dish on taverna menus.

SERVES: 6 for a main course, 12 as a first course

2 pounds large shrimps in the shell ◆ ½ cup extra-virgin olive oil
2 medium yellow onions, finely chopped ◆ 1 plump clove garlic, finely chopped
8 ripe tomatoes, peeled; dice 5, and thinly slice 3 (keep separate)
1 teaspoon honey ◆ 1 teaspoon tomato paste mixed with 2 tablespoons water
4 bay leaves ◆ Small handful of fresh flat-leaf parsley, leaves coarsely chopped
Coarse sea salt and finely cracked pepper to taste
8 ounces feta cheese, cut into 12 slices ◆ 1 tablespoon dried Greek oregano

1 Heat the oven to 350°F.

2 Remove and discard the legs and body shells from the shrimps (leave tail shells in place). With the tip of a small paring knife, devein the shrimps: pull out the black thread passing along the shrimps' backs.

3 Place a heavy sauté pan or skillet over low heat and add 2 tablespoons of the olive oil. Add the shrimps, cover, and cook 4 minutes, occasionally shaking the pan. Transfer the shrimps and pan juices to a bowl, tightly cover, and refrigerate. Wipe the pan with paper towels.

4 Return the sauté pan to low heat and add 3 tablespoons olive oil. Add the onions and cook until soft, about 8 minutes. Add the garlic, diced tomatoes, honey, tomato paste, and bay leaves. Raise the heat to low-medium, and simmer 10 minutes. Add half the parsley and season with a little salt and, more generously, with pepper. Cook, stirring occasionally, until the sauce remains separated for a few seconds when you draw a wooden spoon across the bottom of the pan, about 10 minutes. Add salt and pepper if necessary (the sauce should be highly flavored).

5 Pour the sauce into an ovenproof dish, large enough to hold the shrimps in a single layer, or divide between 6 individual ovenproof dishes. Arrange the shrimps on top, and pour over any juices from the bowl. Cover with the tomato slices, then the feta cheese slices.

6 Sprinkle with oregano, the remaining olive oil, and a little pepper. Bake uncovered 12 minutes.

7 Sprinkle with the rest of the parsley, and serve hot or warm.

NOTE: TO PREPARE THIS DISH AHEAD OF TIME AND BAKE LATER, FOLLOW STEPS 1 THROUGH 5. COVER THE DISH AND REFRIGERATE. TO BAKE, SPRINKLE WITH OREGANO, THE REMAINING OLIVE OIL, AND A LITTLE PEPPER. COVER AND BAKE 10 MINUTES. UNCOVER AND BAKE 10 MINUTES LONGER.

Meatballs in Tomato Sauce

Soutzoukakia

Tasty, colorful soutzoukakia is a legacy of our recent, rather turbulent history. The flavorings are those loved by the Greeks of two generations ago, who used to live in a region that is now part of Turkey. Inexpensive and easy to make, this dish is the perfect weeknight supper. Serve with rice or fried potatoes.

SERVES: 6

1 thick slice good-quality white bread, crust removed ◆ ¾ cup water
1 medium onion, grated ◆ 1 plump clove garlic, finely chopped
2 tablespoons cumin seeds ◆ 2 tablespoons aged red wine vinegar
1 pound lean beef or lamb, finely ground twice
Small bunch of fresh flat-leaf parsley, leaves finely chopped
1 tablespoon dried Greek oregano, crumbled ◆ 1 large egg, lightly beaten
Coarse sea salt and finely cracked pepper to taste ◆ Olive oil for frying

◆

1 Place the bread in a bowl and pour over ½ cup of the water. Set aside for 15 minutes.

2 Combine the onion, garlic, and remaining ¼ cup water in a small saucepan. Bring to a boil and simmer on low heat until the water has evaporated, about 6 minutes (take care not to burn the onion). Set aside.

3 Set a small frying pan over low heat. Add the cumin seeds. Shaking the pan a little, toast the seeds until aromatic, about 1 minute.

4 Transfer to a small mortar or spice grinder and pulverize or grind.

5 With your hand, squeeze out the excess water from the bread. In a large bowl, combine the bread, onion, cumin, vinegar, meat, half the parsley, the oregano, egg, salt, and pepper. Knead this mixture with your hand for few minutes, tightly cover the bowl, and refrigerate until cold.

6 Moisten your hands with cold water. Divide the meat mixture into 18 portions and shape into 2-inch-long patties; flatten slightly.

7 Set a large, heavy sauté pan or skillet over low-medium heat and add olive oil to make a very thin layer. Add enough meat patties to make a single layer in the pan. Cook until browned on both sides, turning once (about 12 minutes). (Use 2 frying pans for greater speed.) Pat dry on paper towels and transfer to a saucepan or skillet large enough to hold the patties in a single layer.

8 Add the remaining parsley to the tomato sauce, stir to mix, and pour over the meat patties. Set over low heat and slowly bring to a boil. Simmer uncovered for 10 minutes. Check the seasonings.

9 Carefully transfer the meat patties to a warm platter and cover with the following sauce.

Tomato Sauce
Saltsa Domatas

For a very quick sauce I warm some olive oil in a skillet, add chopped tomatoes and herbs, and simmer for a few minutes. On other occasions, I like to reduce tomatoes to a rich sauce, as I do here. A tip from my grandmother: add a spoonful of honey to the cooking tomatoes—this turns their natural acidity into a wonderful sweetness.

MAKES: about 2 cups

5 tablespoons extra-virgin olive oil ◆ 1 tablespoon honey ◆ 6 bay leaves 6 ripe medium tomatoes, peeled and diced (reserve juices) ◆ 1 cinnamon stick, broken into large pieces ◆ Coarse sea salt and finely cracked pepper to taste

1 Set a large heavy skillet over low heat and add the olive oil. When warm, add the honey, bay leaves, the tomatoes and their juices, and cinnamon pieces. Raise the heat and bring to a boil. Simmer uncovered 30 to 40 minutes, stirring occasionally.

2 Set a strainer over a medium bowl. Remove the bay leaves and cinnamon pieces from the sauce and discard. Pour the sauce into the strainer and, with the back of a wooden spoon, press the sauce through into the bowl. Season with salt and pepper.

Grilled Marinated Pork

Hirino Skaras

This is a dish I love to make during the harvest. Everyone is working so hard and is so hungry, that only grilled pork seems to satisfy them!

SERVES: 6

6 boneless pork chops or 6 slices of pork loin (about 6 ounces each)
1 tablespoon coarse salt ♦ 1 tablespoon finely cracked pepper
2 tablespoons crushed coriander seeds ♦ 1½ tablespoons honey
3 tablespoons red wine vinegar, plus a few drops more
6 tablespoons extra-virgin olive oil ♦ 1 medium red onion, quartered and thinly sliced
3 tablespoons finely chopped fresh flat-leaf parsley ♦ Large bunch of watercress, sprigs only

♦

1 With your hands, rub the chops with the salt, pepper, and coriander seeds and place in a shallow bowl.

2 In a small bowl, combine the honey, 3 tablespoons vinegar, and 3 tablespoons of the olive oil, and pour this sauce over the chops; turn once or twice to thoroughly coat. Tightly cover the bowl and refrigerate 1 to 3 hours.

3 Heat the broiler or grill.

4 Place the onion in a small bowl and cover with cold water. Set aside.

5 Transfer the chops to a broiler tray or grill pan; reserve any marinade. Brush the chops with the remaining olive oil and broil or grill on both sides until browned. Baste liberally with the rest of the marinade. Lower the heat and continue cooking the chops, turning once until done, about 15 minutes. Continue to baste frequently.

6 Squeeze the onion between paper towels to remove any excess water, and place in a dry bowl. Sprinkle with the few drops of vinegar and the parsley; toss to mix.

7 Spread the watercress over a platter. Arrange the chops over the greens and top with the onion-parsley mixture.

Pork and Greens in the Oven
Hirino me Horta sto Fourno

*I make this roast on the occasions when we fire up our wood-burning oven, and
I like to bake it for several hours—the meat is soft enough to eat with a spoon!
But it can be very successfully baked in your home oven also.*

SERVES: 6

One 3-pound boneless pork rib roast, fat trimmed to a thin layer
Coarse sea salt and finely cracked pepper to taste
3 tablespoons Hymettus or other strongly flavored honey
Juice of 1 lemon ♦ 1 tablespoon ground coriander ♦ 1 teaspoon ground cumin
½ cup extra-virgin olive oil ♦ 2 tablespoons dried Greek oregano
2 tablespoons dried sage, crumbled ♦ 1 cup dry white wine, meat broth, or water
2 bunches of arugula, large leaves torn into pieces, or purslane, sprigs only

1 Place the pork, fat side up, in a heavy baking dish or roasting pan. Rub with salt and pepper.

2 In a small bowl, whisk together the honey, lemon juice, coriander, cumin, and half the olive oil. Pour this over the pork, cover with aluminum foil, and set aside (preferably not in the refrigerator) for 1 hour; baste occasionally.

3 Heat the oven to 375°F.

4 Pour the remaining ¼ cup olive oil over the pork, and sprinkle with the oregano and sage. Pour half the wine into the dish and bake 20 minutes; baste the pork several times.

Pour the remaining wine into the dish, and bake 1 hour longer until the pork is cooked. (A roasting thermometer inserted into the pork should read 150°F to 155°F.) Baste once or twice, and add a little wine or water if it appears dry.

5 Transfer the pork to a cutting board, cut into serving slices, and cover with foil to keep warm.

6 Place the baking dish over low heat. Add the arugula and stir around the dish with a wooden spoon until it becomes a little wilted, about 1 minute. Spread over a warm platter and season with salt and pepper. Arrange the pork slices on top and pour over any pan juices.

chapter four
VEGETABLES
& SALADS

Braised Artichokes

Aginares

In our household, we reserve special affection for spring vegetables. We do try to observe the long Lent fast, but as we lose our older generation, it becomes more and more difficult to do, for there are so many good foods that we are not allowed to eat. However, the utterly delicious flavors of these beautiful new vegetables help us through.

SERVES: 6 as a side dish, 12 for a first course

1 organic lemon, juiced; reserve halves ◆ 1 tablespoon all-purpose flour
1 teaspoon coarse sea salt plus more to taste ◆ 6 large fresh artichokes
12 tiny new potatoes, scrubbed
½ cup extra-virgin olive oil or to taste
8 green onions, including unblemished green parts, trimmed and cut into diagonal slivers
4 large ripe tomatoes, peeled and diced (reserve juices) ◆ ½ teaspoon sugar
1½ cups fresh shelled peas ◆ Freshly ground pepper to taste
12 small sprigs of fresh fennel

◆

1 Prepare a large bowl three quarters full of iced water. Add the lemon juice and whisk in the flour and 1 teaspoon salt (flour and salt help prevent the artichokes from discoloring).

2 Discard the outer leaves of the artichokes, leaving only the tender light green ones. With a sharp knife, slice off the top third of each artichoke and trim any stems to 1 inch. Using a small spoon, scoop out the fuzzy chokes. Cut into quarters, rinse, rub with

a lemon half, and add to the bowl of iced water. When you have prepared all the artichokes, add the lemon halves to the bowl.

3 Fill a large saucepan with 2 inches water and bring to a boil. Drain the artichoke hearts, and add to the pan with the potatoes. Bring back to a boil, reduce the heat to low, and simmer 6 minutes. Drain over a bowl; reserve 2 cups of the cooking liquid.

4 Set a large, heavy saucepan over low heat and add 3 tablespoons of the olive oil. Add the green onions, the tomatoes and their juices, and sugar. Cook 5 minutes, stirring occasionally with a wooden spoon. Add the peas, artichokes, potatoes, and half of the reserved cooking liquid or enough to barely cover the vegetables. Season with salt and pepper, cover the pan, and simmer 25 minutes or until the artichokes and potatoes are just tender. Check occasionally to make sure that there is still a little liquid in the pan; add more of the reserved cooking liquid if needed.

5 Transfer the vegetables and sauce to a shallow serving bowl. Pour over the remaining olive oil, and check the seasonings. Garnish with fennel and serve hot, warm, or at room temperature.

Purslane Salad

Glystritha Salatika

Purslane is a weed that pops up everywhere in my garden. Weed or not, it's very good for you, and its light lemony flavor is utterly delicious. You can find it at local farmers' markets or in specialty produce stores.

SERVES: 6

9 cups purslane sprigs ◆ Juice of ½ small lemon
6 to 8 tablespoons extra-virgin olive oil to taste ◆ Coarse sea salt to taste

1 Thoroughly wash the purslane sprigs in cold water. Drain and spin or pat dry. (Don't waste any tender stems—either coarsely chop them and add to the salad or save them to use in a soup.) Transfer to a serving bowl.

2 In a small bowl, whisk together the lemon juice and olive oil. Pour this sauce over the purslane, sprinkle with salt, and serve.

Asparagus with Honey Vinegar Sauce
Sparangia Lathoxsithi

The season for asparagus is so short that I relish every moment I am able to prepare it for the table. Sometimes I let my husband grill our asparagus alongside other vegetables or meats. Usually, however, I simply cook the slender stems for a few minutes, and serve them as a side dish to grilled meats or as a light lunch dish or meze with a sauce made from our best local olive oil and honey.

SERVES: 6 for a side dish, 10 as a meze

20 asparagus stems (about 12 ounces), rinsed
½ tablespoon Hymettus or other strongly flavored honey ♦ 1 tablespoon red wine vinegar
5 tablespoons extra-virgin olive oil ♦ Coarse sea salt and finely cracked pepper to taste
Small sprigs of fresh chervil or 2 tablespoons finely chopped fresh flat-leaf parsley

♦

1 Fill a large sauté pan or skillet with 1 inch water and bring to a boil. Break off each asparagus stem at the lowest point where it easily snaps.

2 Add the asparagus to the pan, and simmer over low heat until just tender (slender stems, about 2 minutes; thicker stems, 3 to 4 minutes). Drain and spread on paper towels to dry.

3 In a large, shallow bowl, combine the honey and vinegar and whisk in the olive oil. Add the asparagus and carefully turn in the marinade. Cover the bowl and set aside for 1 hour at room temperature (or refrigerate if you prefer).

4 Transfer the asparagus to a platter, and cover with the marinade. Sprinkle with salt and pepper, and garnish with chervil (or parsley).

Black-Eyed Peas and Watercress
Mavromatika me Karthamo

This recipe provides me with yet another way I can include protein-rich dried beans in our diet. Although I use watercress here, you might like to try arugula, purslane, endive lettuce, young beet greens, or other horta instead. Serve with slices of cheese and bowls of olives.

SERVES: 6

4 large ripe tomatoes, peeled and diced (reserve juices) ◆ Large pinch of sugar
1 cup dried black-eyed peas, soaked 6 hours or overnight covered in cold water
½ tablespoon Hymettus or other strongly flavored honey ◆ 1 tablespoon red wine vinegar
1 tablespoon dried Greek oregano, crumbled ◆ 6 tablespoons extra-virgin olive oil
Coarse sea salt and finely cracked pepper to taste
8 green onions, including unblemished green parts, trimmed and cut into
thin diagonal slivers ◆ Large bunch of watercress, sprigs only

◆

1 Sprinkle the tomatoes with sugar and set aside.

2 Drain the peas, transfer to a large saucepan, and add cold water to cover. Bring to a boil, drain, and rinse out the saucepan. Return the peas to the pan and add cold water to cover by 3 inches, and bring to a boil over medium heat. Cover, reduce the heat to low, and simmer 20 minutes or until just tender. Drain in a colander. Set aside for a few minutes to dry.

3 In a large bowl, combine the honey, vinegar, and oregano, and whisk in the olive oil. Add the peas, salt, and pepper, and gently stir to mix. Add more salt and pepper if desired. Carefully stir in the green onions and tomatoes.

4 Line a platter or shallow bowl with the watercress. Pile the peas and tomatoes on top and serve.

White Bean Salad

Fassolia me Karotta ke Elies

I like to cook a pot of beans whenever I'm in the kitchen for a few hours. The next day, I simply add vegetables and herbs to the beans and I have a nutritious salad.

SERVES: 6

1 cup dried cannellini or northern beans, soaked 6 hours or overnight covered in cold water ◆ 1 medium yellow onion, peeled and stuck with 2 cloves
7 tablespoons extra-virgin olive oil ◆ Juice of 1 small lemon
Coarse sea salt and finely cracked pepper to taste ◆ 6 small, young carrots, scrubbed or peeled and cut thinly or sliced diagonally ◆ 1 tablespoon capers, rinsed and patted dry
2 anchovy fillets, rinsed and patted dry ◆ Small handful of fresh flat-leaf parsley, leaves finely chopped ◆ 4 tablespoons cilantro, chopped
1 dozen Greek olives, drained ◆ 1 small red onion, cut into very thin rings

◆

1 Drain the beans, transfer to a saucepan, and add cold water to cover. Bring to a boil over medium heat, drain, and rinse out the saucepan.

2 Return the beans to the saucepan. Add the onion, and water to cover by 4 inches. Bring to a boil over medium heat, cover, reduce the heat to low, and simmer 40 minutes or until the beans are just tender. Drain in a colander and set aside for a few minutes to dry.

3 In a large bowl, combine the beans, 3 tablespoons of the olive oil, half the lemon juice, salt, and pepper. Gently stir to mix, cover, and set aside.

4 Set a heavy saucepan over medium heat. Add 2 inches water and bring to a boil. Add the carrots and cook until just tender (6 minutes). Drain.

5 Place the capers and anchovy fillets in a mortar or small bowl. Using a pestle or wooden spoon, pound together until mashed. Whisk in the remaining lemon juice and olive oil, and stir in half the parsley and the cilantro. Gently stir this sauce into the beans. Add the carrots and olives, carefully stir to mix, and check the seasonings.

6 Transfer to a platter. Sprinkle with the red onion and remaining parsley. Serve at room temperature.

Giant Beans
Gigantes Plaki

Keep this dish in mind when you invite a large group of friends or relatives to lunch or supper. With cheese, bread, and a large green salad on the table, gigantes plaki easily expands to feed extra guests. Should you have any left over, you will have an excellent meze or light lunch already prepared for the next day.

SERVES: 6

2 cups dried large lima beans or butter beans, soaked overnight in plenty of water
5 tablespoons extra-virgin olive oil ◆ 1 large onion, quartered and thinly sliced
2 medium carrots, peeled or scrubbed and thinly sliced
2 ripe medium tomatoes, peeled and diced (reserve juices)
1 teaspoon honey ◆ 1 tablespoon tomato paste mixed with 2 tablespoons water
1 tablespoon ground coriander ◆ 4 bay leaves ◆ 1 plump clove garlic, finely chopped
5 tablespoons finely chopped fresh flat-leaf parsley ◆ 2 tablespoons dried Greek oregano
Coarse sea salt and finely cracked pepper to taste ◆ Juice of ½ small lemon

◆

1 Drain the beans and place in a large saucepan with water to cover by 5 inches. Bring to a boil over medium heat. Reduce the heat to low and simmer 30 minutes or until just tender. Drain.

2 Heat the oven to 350°F.

3 Place a large, heavy saucepan over low heat and add half the olive oil. When warm, add the onion and the carrots, and cook until the onions are soft (about 10 minutes); stir occasionally with a wooden spoon. Add the tomatoes and their juices, the honey, tomato paste, coriander, bay leaves, garlic, half the parsley, and the oregano, and stir to mix. Simmer 10 minutes.

4 Choose a heavy baking dish or casserole. Add the beans and tomato sauce and gently stir to mix. Season generously with salt and pepper, and pour over the remaining olive oil. Loosely cover the dish with aluminum foil, and bake 45 minutes. Remove the foil and continue baking 15 to 30 minutes longer or until the top of the beans is slightly crusty.

5 Sprinkle with lemon juice and the remaining parsley, and serve warm or at room temperature.

Beets and Beet Greens
Panzaria Salatika

All you need for this simple, delicious dish are three top-quality ingredients—fresh beets, pulled from the ground just as you need them (or, if store-bought, still with their crisp, deep-green leaves in place), a good Greek olive oil, and iodine-rich sea salt. Serve as a side dish to meats or fish, or with slices of feta cheese and bowls of olives for lunch or supper.

SERVES: 6

8 small beets, with their leaves ◆ **6 tablespoons extra-virgin olive oil**
1½ tablespoons red wine vinegar ◆ **Coarse sea salt and finely cracked pepper to taste**

◆

1 Trim the stems and root ends from the beets; reserve the green leaves. Using a stiff brush, thoroughly scrub the beets under cold running water. Cut into quarters or large, bite-sized pieces.

2 Strip the leaves from the stems. Discard any thick or tough stems and cut the remainder into 1- to 2-inch-long pieces. Wash the leaves and tear into large pieces.

3 Half fill a large saucepan with water and bring to a boil. Add the beets and cook for 15 minutes or until just barely tender (to check, pierce with the point of a small knife). Add the stems and cook 3 minutes longer. Drain, and transfer the beets and stems to a bowl. Set aside to cool.

4 Using a small paring knife, remove the skins from the beets, being careful to catch any juices in the bowl.

5 Place a large sauté pan or skillet over low heat and add 2 tablespoons of the olive oil. Add the greens and cook, stirring with a wooden spoon, until just wilted (about 4 minutes).

6 In a small bowl, whisk together the vinegar and remaining olive oil. Pour this sauce over the beets, and gently toss to mix. Transfer to one side of a platter, sprinkle with salt and pepper, and top with any sauce remaining in the bowl. Arrange the greens beside the beets. Serve warm or at room temperature.

Romaine Lettuce Salad

Marouli Salatika

This is the true salad of spring and the one we like to have on our Easter table. Early in the year, the romaine lettuces in our garden are tender and sweet. Later, when their flavor is stronger, we use only the lettuce hearts. But we don't waste the outer leaves—they are perfect in Chicken Fricassée (see page 63).

SERVES: 6

2 heads young romaine lettuce ◆ **6 green onions, including unblemished green parts, trimmed and cut into thin diagonal slivers**
12 sprigs of fresh dill, coarsely chopped
12 sprigs of fresh flat-leaf parsley, leaves coarsely chopped
1 to 2 tablespoons freshly squeezed lemon juice (to taste)
6 tablespoons extra-virgin olive oil or to taste ◆ **Coarse sea salt to taste**

◆

1 Separate the leaves of the lettuce from the heads; discard any large stems and blemished leaves. Rinse well and spin or pat dry.

2 Make a small stack of leaves by placing them one on top of the other; roll into a tight cigar. Holding the roll firmly under one hand, slice into ¼-inch-wide ribbons. Combine the lettuce, green onions, dill, and parsley in a serving bowl.

3 In a small bowl, whisk together the lemon juice and olive oil. Pour this sauce over the greens, toss together, and sprinkle with salt. Serve immediately.

Mama says...
If you love the flavor of salt but want to limit your intake, use coarse sea salt—toss greens in latholemono (olive oil and lemon juice sauce) before sprinkling with salt. The oil prevents the salt from dissolving into the leaves.

Fava Beans and Cracked Wheat Salad
Pligouri ke Fava

*Fava beans are in season for only a few short weeks during early spring.
We enjoy the youngest, most tender ones raw, as a meze, or in salads such as this
one. Serve with yogurt or slices of feta cheese.*

SERVES: 6

1 cup cracked wheat ◆ Coarse sea salt ◆ Juice of 1 small lemon
5 cups young, fresh, podded fava beans ◆ ½ cup extra-virgin olive oil
Finely cracked pepper ◆ 8 green onions, including unblemished green parts,
trimmed and cut into thin diagonal slivers
Small handful of young arugula leaves, torn into small pieces if large,
or purslane, broken into sprigs ◆ 3 tablespoons finely chopped fresh flat-leaf parsley

◆

1 Put the cracked wheat in a bowl and cover with cold water. Stir in a large pinch of salt and a generous squeeze of the lemon juice. Set aside 30 minutes; stir once or twice.

2 Steam the beans, or simmer in a little water for 3 to 5 minutes, until just tender. Drain, and set aside.

3 In a large bowl, whisk together the olive oil and remaining lemon juice. Drain the cracked wheat, and dry between paper towels. Add to the bowl with the fava beans, and salt and pepper to taste. Gently mix together, without breaking the beans. Lightly mix in the green onions, arugula (or purslane), and parsley.

4 Transfer to a shallow serving bowl or platter.

Green Beans in Tomato Sauce

Fassolia Lathera

*Lathera dishes (vegetables slow-cooked with plenty of olive oil) are a specialty of
Peloponnese kitchens. All sorts of vegetables can be prepared this way, including
okra, artichokes, potatoes, cauliflower florets, eggplants, zucchini, and even
cooked dried beans. Serve warm as a side dish to meat or fish,
or cold with olives, cheese, and crusty bread.*

SERVES: 6

7 tablespoons extra-virgin olive oil or more to taste
2 medium mild onions, quartered and thinly sliced ◆ 1 clove garlic, finely chopped
1 teaspoon ground coriander ◆ 5 ripe medium tomatoes, peeled and diced (reserve juices)
1 teaspoon honey or sugar ◆ 1 tablespoon tomato paste mixed with 2 tablespoons water
Coarse sea salt and finely cracked pepper to taste
1½ pounds fresh green beans, trimmed and cut in 3-inch-long pieces
Small bunch of fresh flat-leaf parsley, leaves chopped ◆ Juice of ½ a small lemon

◆

1 Set a large, heavy sauté pan or skillet over low heat. Add 3 tablespoons olive oil. Sauté the onions 10 minutes or until soft, stirring occasionally.

2 Add the garlic and coriander and cook until their aromas rise, about 1 minute. Add the tomatoes and their juices, honey, tomato paste, salt, and pepper. Raise the heat to low-medium, gently stir to mix, and bring to a low boil. Reduce the heat to low and simmer uncovered for 15 minutes or until the sauce stays divided a second or two when you draw a wooden spoon across the bottom of the pan.

3 Steam the beans for 5 minutes or lightly boil for 3 minutes. Drain. Add the beans, the remaining olive oil, and half the parsley to the tomato sauce. Cover the pan and, holding the cover in place, firmly shake the pan to mix everything together. Continue cooking over low heat for 15 minutes or until the beans are tender. Set aside, with cover in place, to cool slightly. Check the seasonings.

4 Transfer the beans and sauce to a shallow serving dish, and sprinkle with lemon juice and the rest of the parsley.

Slow-Baked Zucchini

Kolokithaki sto Fourno

Make this simple, versatile dish on the days when you are already using your oven. It takes only minutes to prepare, and it can be served hot, warm, or at room temperature. Bear in mind that the length of time needed to cook whole zucchini depends on their diameter, not on their length, so choose ones of similar size for this recipe.

SERVES: 6

18 small zucchini, 1 inch to 1½ inches in diameter
5 tablespoons extra-virgin olive oil ◆ 6 tablespoons cold water ◆ Juice of 1 small lemon
Coarse sea salt and finely cracked pepper ◆ 1 tablespoon dried Greek oregano, crumbled

◆

1 Heat the oven to 325°F.

2 Trim the zucchini and rinse. Arrange in a single layer in a heavy, shallow baking dish just large enough to easily hold them. Pour over the olive oil, water, and half the lemon juice. Lightly cover the dish with aluminum foil and bake 40 minutes or until the zucchini are barely soft; roll them around in the cooking liquid once or twice. (Add a few tablespoons water if the dish appears to be drying out.)

3 Transfer the zucchini to a warm platter and pour over the cooking liquid. Sprinkle with the remaining lemon juice, salt and pepper to taste, and the oregano.

Mama says...
For a quick meze the following day, bake a few extra zucchini. (They may be refrigerated in their cooking liquid in a covered dish for up to 36 hours.) To serve, slice crosswise, and sprinkle with coarse sea salt, finely cracked pepper, dried Greek oregano, lemon juice, and olive oil to taste.

Winter Cabbage Salad
Lakhanosalata

Crisp, crunchy white cabbage and bright orange carrots make perfect partners for some of my favorite ingredients—feta cheese, olives, olive oil, and rigani (dried Greek oregano)—in this easy-to-make, pretty winter salad. Sometimes I add a few shredded arugula leaves, or other herbs such as fennel, chervil, or cilantro.

SERVES: 6

1 small head white cabbage (about 1 pound) ◆ 1 small clove garlic
½ teaspoon coarse sea salt ◆ 1½ tablespoons red wine vinegar
6 to 8 tablespoons extra-virgin olive oil (to taste) ◆ 2 medium carrots, peeled
6 green onions, including unblemished green parts
Small handful of fresh flat-leaf parsley, leaves chopped ◆ 12 Greek black olives, drained
1 cup feta cheese, drained and crumbled into large pieces
Finely cracked pepper to taste ◆ 1 tablespoon dried Greek oregano, crumbled

◆

1 Remove and discard the outer cabbage leaves. Rinse the cabbage head, cut into quarters, and core. Slice very thinly or shred using a large-holed grater. Transfer to a large bowl.

2 Place the garlic and salt in a mortar. Using a pestle or wooden spoon, pound together until well mashed. Stir in the vinegar and 2 tablespoons olive oil. Pour this sauce over the cabbage, stir to mix, and set aside 15 minutes.

3 Using a mandolin or large-holed grater, finely julienne or shred the carrots. Cut the green onions into thin, diagonal slivers. Add the carrots, green onions, half the parsley, and the remaining olive oil to the cabbage, and lightly stir to mix.

4 Transfer to a serving dish. Top with the olives and feta cheese, and sprinkle with pepper, oregano, and the rest of the parsley.

Fried Cauliflower

Kounoupithi

Although I like my cauliflower served very simply—warm, in small florets, with olive oil and lemon juice poured over them at the table—everyone else in my house prefers to have it fried. I use olive oil to fry the cauliflower, but any good oil suitable for deep-fat frying could be used instead. Serve piping hot, with a wild arugula salad.

SERVES: 6

¾ **cup all-purpose flour** ◆ **2 tablespoons chickpea flour**
Sea salt and freshly ground pepper to taste ◆ **1 large egg, separated**
½ **cup beer or water** ◆ **1 large head of cauliflower** ◆ **Oil for frying** ◆ **Lemon wedges**

◆

1 Heat the oven to 130°F and warm a platter.

2 In a bowl, combine the all-purpose flour, chickpea flour, salt, and pepper. Stir in the egg yolk and beer.

3 In a medium bowl, whisk the egg white until thick, but not stiff, and stir into the batter. Add a little water if necessary to thin the batter to the consistency of pouring cream. Tightly cover the bowl and refrigerate 30 minutes.

4 Discard the leaves and tough stems from the cauliflower and separate into florets. Cut the florets into large bite-sized pieces and trim off excess stems.

5 Half fill a medium saucepan with water and bring to a boil. Cook the florets until just tender, about 4 minutes. Drain in a colander and set aside.

6 Set a heavy sauté pan or skillet over low heat and add oil to make a ½-inch-deep layer (or use a deep-fat fryer); slowly bring to just below smoking temperature. The oil is hot enough to use when you drop in a little of the batter and it immediately sizzles.

7 Dip the florets in the batter, a few at one time, and fry until golden brown. Remove with a slotted spoon, drain on paper towels, and transfer to the warm platter. Keep warm in the oven while you fry the remaining florets. Serve with lemon wedges.

Baked Eggplants in Grape Leaves
Melitzanes sto Fourno

Make this colorful dish for a gathering of friends or family. The grape leaves act as a lid, protecting the eggplants from the oven's heat, and lend a delicate, lemony fragrance to the filling. They are not eaten, so you can use larger, or tougher, leaves instead of the more tender ones (keep these for Tiny Stuffed Grape Leaves, page 26). Perfect for casual entertaining, this dish tastes even better when made a day ahead—the flavors mellow and deepen. Serve warm or at room temperature for a first course or hot as a side dish for grilled meats.

SERVES: 6 for a side dish, or 12 as a first course

12 small eggplants, about 4-inch long or 6 medium eggplants
Coarse sea salt to taste ◆ ¾ cup extra-virgin olive oil
3 medium onions, quartered and thinly sliced ◆ 1 plump clove garlic, finely chopped
4 ripe medium tomatoes, peeled and diced (reserve juices)
⅓ packed cup currants or small dark seedless raisins
1 teaspoon ground cinnamon
Large handful of fresh flat-leaf parsley, leaves finely chopped
2 tablespoons dried Greek oregano ◆ Finely cracked pepper to taste
1½ cups cooked rice (made from ½ cup raw short-grained white rice)
Enough fresh or brine-preserved grape leaves to make 2 layers in the baking dish; blanch preserved leaves 3 seconds, fresh leaves 5 seconds; and drain between paper towels
1 tablespoon honey ◆ 2 tablespoons red wine vinegar

◆

1 Trim off the stem end of each eggplant and cut lengthwise in half. Arrange on a plate, sprinkle the cut sides of the eggplants with salt, and set aside for 30 minutes to sweat.

2 Place a heavy skillet or frying pan over low heat and add 3 tablespoons of the olive oil. Add the onions and cook until very soft, about 15 minutes; stir occasionally. Add the garlic and the tomatoes and their juices, raise the heat to low-medium, and simmer until most of the liquid has evaporated, about 10 minutes. Stir in the currants, cinnamon, most of the parsley, half the oregano, salt, pepper, and rice.

3 Heat the oven to 325°F.

4 Dry the eggplants with paper towels. Place a large, heavy skillet or frying pan over low-medium heat and add 3 tablespoons olive oil. When hot, fry half the eggplants, turning once, until the cut sides are a deep golden brown and the skin sides dark and wrinkled, about 10 minutes. Drain on paper towels. Add 2 tablespoons olive oil to the skillet, repeat with the remaining eggplants, and drain on paper towels.

5 With a small spoon, scoop out the eggplant centers onto a board, leaving ¼-inch-thick shells. Discard most of the seeds, finely dice the flesh, and stir into the rice mixture.

6 Line a heavy baking dish, just large enough to hold the eggplants in a single layer, with half the grape leaves, glossy sides down. Arrange the eggplant shells in the dish and divide the rice mixture between them, heaping it a little in the center.

7 In a small bowl, whisk together the honey, vinegar, and 2 tablespoons olive oil. Pour this sauce over the eggplants. Lightly cover the eggplants with the remaining grape leaves, glossy sides down. Pour ½ cup water into the dish and bake uncovered for 1 hour. Check occasionally and add a little more water to the dish if it appears dry.

8 Discard the top layer of grape leaves. With a spatula, transfer the eggplants to a platter or to individual plates. Discard the remaining grape leaves. Spoon over any cooking liquid remaining in the dish, check the seasonings, and sprinkle with the rest of the olive oil and parsley.

Marinated Mushrooms
Manitaria Marinata

There are plenty of mushrooms in the woods on the hills surrounding our house. Most of my neighbors don't like to pick them, as they all seem to know someone who has died from eating a mushroom! But I know which ones to look for, and I never have to search too hard. Delicious with grilled meats or bean dishes, you can prepare manitaria marinata a day ahead, but bring back to room temperature for serving.

SERVES: 6

5 cups small closed-cap field mushrooms ◆ 3 tablespoons extra-virgin olive oil
4 bay leaves ◆ 1 tablespoon coriander seeds, crushed ◆ ½ cup dry white wine
1 shallot, finely chopped ◆ 2 tablespoons chopped fresh flat-leaf parsley
2 tablespoons cilantro ◆ Coarse sea salt and finely cracked pepper to taste

◆

1 Trim the mushrooms and brush or wipe clean; cut the larger ones in half.

2 Place a heavy saucepan over low heat and add the olive oil, bay leaves, and coriander seeds. When warm, add the mushrooms, cover, and reduce the heat to very low. Cook (sweat) the mushrooms for 6 minutes or until they have released some of their water, but are still firm. Transfer to a bowl.

3 Place a small pan over low heat, add the wine, and bring to a boil. Pour over the mushrooms and set aside to cool. (If leaving longer than a few hours, cover and refrigerate.)

4 Transfer the mushrooms to a serving dish.

5 On a board, chop together the shallots, parsley, cilantro, salt, and pepper. Scatter this mixture over the mushrooms and serve.

Potatoes with Olive Oil and Lemon
Patates Lemonatas

*For this recipe, choose potatoes that stay firm when roasted, and make patates
lemonatas when you are already using your oven for something else.
Bake more than you need—potatoes cooked this way are a delicious meze
when served cold, with ouzo, a Greek spirit.*

SERVES: 6

**6 large roasting potatoes ◆ ½ cup extra-virgin olive oil or more if needed
2 tablespoons dried Greek oregano ◆ Coarse sea salt and finely cracked pepper to taste
Juice of 2 lemons**

◆

1 Heat the oven to 375°F.

2 Peel the potatoes, and cut lengthwise into
large pieces. Arrange in a heavy baking dish, just
large enough to hold them in a single layer.
Pour over the olive oil and enough water to
make a thin layer in the dish. Sprinkle with
oregano, salt, and pepper.

3 Bake uncovered for 45 minutes or until the
potatoes are just tender; if the dish appears dry,
add a little water. Pour over the lemon juice,
baste the potatoes with the pan juices, and return
the dish to the oven for 15 minutes.

4 Add salt and pepper if necessary. Serve hot,
warm, or at room temperature.

Stuffed Tomatoes
Domates Yemistes

Every Sunday, my family comes together for a long, relaxing lunch. I use my tapsi, a huge, round baking pan, to cook the food. I cook everything ahead of time and, if extra friends or neighbors turn up, there's always enough for them, too. When our own luscious tomatoes are ready to pick, this dish is my favorite way of preparing them. Serve hot, warm, or at room temperature.

SERVES: 6 for a side dish, or 12 as a first course

6 very large, or 12 medium-large, tomatoes ◆ Fine sea salt to taste
½ cup extra-virgin olive oil or more to taste ◆ 1 medium onion, grated
1 teaspoon sugar ◆ ½ cup short-grained white rice
4 tablespoons cracked wheat, soaked 30 minutes covered in cold water
⅓ cup pine nuts, lightly toasted ◆ 2 tablespoons dried Greek oregano, crumbled
⅓ packed cup currants or small dark seedless raisins ◆ Freshly ground pepper to taste
Small bunch of fresh flat-leaf parsley, leaves finely chopped
3 medium potatoes (choose ones suitable for roasting), peeled ◆ Lemon wedges

◆

1 Heat the oven to 350°F. Choose a baking dish with sides at least 2 inches deep, and large enough to hold tomatoes and potatoes in a single layer.

2 Slice the tops off the tomatoes and set aside to use as lids later. With a small spoon, scoop out as much of the pulp as possible without breaking the tomatoes. Discard the seeds and dice the pulp; set aside with the juices. Arrange the tomato shells in the baking dish and sprinkle a large pinch of salt inside each one.

3 Place a heavy saucepan over low heat. When warm, add 3 tablespoons olive oil and the onion and cook until soft, about 8 minutes; stir occasionally. Add the tomato pulp and juices, sugar, salt to taste, the rice, and ¾ cup water. Bring to a low boil and simmer 10 minutes or until the liquid has evaporated.

4 Squeeze the cracked wheat between paper towels. Using a fork, stir the cracked wheat, pine nuts, oregano, currants, pepper, and most of the

parsley into the rice. Check the seasonings; the filling should be well flavored. Fill the tomatoes with the rice mixture and replace their tops to make lids.

5 Cut the potatoes lengthwise into large pieces and arrange between the tomatoes; sprinkle with salt and pepper. Pour the remaining olive oil over both the potatoes and tomatoes, and add water if necessary to make a thin layer of liquid in the dish. Bake uncovered for 30 minutes. Carefully turn the potatoes and bake 15 to 30 minutes longer or until the tomatoes are browned and very soft.

6 Sprinkle with salt and pepper to taste, and the remaining parsley, and serve from the dish. Have a bowl of lemon wedges on the table, too.

Young Zucchini Salad
Kolokithakia Salata

One of the great advantages of having a vegetable garden is that we can have the most beautiful, tiny zucchini, straight from the plant, as a simple salad. This dish may be served warm or at room temperature, either with slices of feta cheese as a first course or as a side dish to meats.

SERVES: 6

**18 small zucchini, about 3 inches long ◆ Juice of ½ small lemon or to taste
6 tablespoons extra-virgin olive oil ◆ Coarse sea salt and finely cracked pepper to taste**

1 Trim any tough stems from the zucchini; leave the tender stems intact.

2 Half fill a large saucepan with water and bring to a boil. Add the zucchini and lightly boil for 5 to 8 minutes or until tender (but not soft); drain.

3 Transfer to a platter or serving bowl. Squeeze the lemon juice over, pour the olive oil over, and sprinkle with salt and pepper.

Country-Style Salad
Khoriatiki Salata

The ubiquitous Greek salad that's featured on every tourist taverna menu is based on the simple ingredients we village cooks have available to us throughout the summer. This is why we call it khoriatiki (country-style) salad. Our homemade Greek salad is far nicer than any you will find in a taverna.

SERVES: 6

4 large ripe tomatoes, peeled if desired ◆ ½ teaspoon sugar ◆ Coarse sea salt to taste
1 large English cucumber, peeled, halved lengthwise, and cut into half-moons
1 medium bell pepper, any color, roasted and skinned, seeds wiped off, and cut lengthwise into thin slices ◆ Large handful of purslane or watercress, sprigs only, or a small handful of arugula or young romaine lettuce leaves, torn into pieces
1⅓ cups feta cheese, drained, and crumbled into large pieces
1 small red onion, thinly sliced
12 Greek black olives such as kalamatas or Thasos, drained
6 to 8 tablespoons extra-virgin olive oil (to taste) ◆ Finely cracked pepper to taste
2 tablespoons dried Greek oregano, crumbled

◆

1 Using a small, sharp knife, core the tomatoes and cut into wedges. Sprinkle with sugar and salt, and set aside.

2 In a large bowl, gently combine the cucumber, bell pepper slices, and purslane.

3 Transfer to a serving platter, and scatter over the tomatoes, feta cheese, onion, and olives. Pour over the olive oil, and sprinkle with pepper, oregano, and more salt if desired.

chapter five

EGGS, PASTA
& PILAFS

Herb Omelet

Omeleta me Votana

If you have very fresh eggs and a handful of just-picked herbs, you can make an omelet just like mine. I like to mix together spinach and tender young sprigs of purslane, or watercress, parsley, and chives. Serve with olives and slices of feta cheese.

SERVES: 1

3 free-range eggs ◆ 2 tablespoons extra-virgin olive oil
Leaves from a small handful of watercress (about ⅔ cup)
2 tablespoons finely chopped fresh flat-leaf parsley ◆ 1 tablespoon unsalted butter
Coarse sea salt and finely cracked pepper to taste ◆ 2 tablespoons chopped chives

◆

1 Break the eggs into a bowl and beat well with two forks or a small whisk.

2 Place a seasoned 8-inch omelet pan, or a skillet with rounded sides, over low heat. When very warm, add the olive oil, watercress, and parsley and stir with a wooden spoon until the watercress is wilted, about 1 minute.

3 Add the butter, and tilt the pan to distribute evenly. Raise the heat a little, and pour in the eggs. Gently tilt the pan as the omelet cooks, and lift the edges of the setting egg with a spatula to let the still-runny egg slide underneath. When the eggs are set, slide the spatula under one side of the omelet and gently flick it over to make a half-moon.

4 Slide the omelet onto a warm plate and sprinkle with salt, pepper, and chives.

Mama says... You will find an omelet much easier to make if you use a seasoned omelet pan or skillet: sprinkle 2 tablespoons salt over the bottom of the pan and set over low heat for 5 minutes. The salt will slowly turn pale brown as it absorbs all the matter that is invariably left in the pan. Discard the salt, and thoroughly wipe the pan with paper towels.

Potato and Sweet Pepper Omelet
Sfongata

This is one of my standby lunch or supper dishes for those days when everyone is in a hurry. I've used potatoes and peppers here, but you can substitute other vegetables such as zucchini, eggplants, asparagus, onions, beans, or leeks, or even vegetables left over from a meal the day before. Serve with crusty bread and wild greens.

SERVES: 2

3 tablespoons extra-virgin olive oil ◆ 1 tablespoon unsalted butter
3 small potatoes, cooked, and cut into ¾-inch dice ◆ 1 bell pepper (any color), scorched, skin rubbed off, seeds and seed box discarded
Coarse sea salt and finely cracked pepper to taste ◆ 4 large free-range eggs
3 tablespoons finely grated kephalotyri, kasseri, or parmesan cheese
3 tablespoons chopped fresh flat-leaf parsley or chervil or a mixture
6 small Greek black olives, drained

◆

1 Heat the broiler or grill.

2 Place a seasoned 9-inch omelet pan or heavy skillet with rounded sides over low heat. When very warm, add the olive oil and butter. When the butter is melted, add the potato cubes, and spread evenly around the pan. Sauté over low heat for about 8 minutes or until pale golden brown on all sides.

3 Cut the bell pepper lengthwise into thin slices, add to the pan, and use the spatula to distribute evenly; cook for a few minutes. Season with salt and pepper.

4 Break the eggs into a bowl, and beat with two forks or a wire whisk. Run the spatula under the potatoes to loosen from the bottom of the pan. Raise the heat a little, pour in the eggs, and tilt the pan to distribute evenly. Sprinkle with the cheese. Gently tilt the pan as the omelet cooks, and lift the edges with a spatula to let the still-runny egg slide underneath. When almost set, place the pan under the broiler. Cook until the top is set and slightly browned; if necessary, turn the pan under the broiler to brown evenly.

5 Sprinkle with parsley and olives and serve from the pan.

Chicken with Tiny Square Pasta

Kotopoulo me Hilopites

If you can't find tiny square pasta (hilopites), use orzo instead. Both do the trick of absorbing the flavorful sauce. Serve with horta or Slow-Baked Zucchini (see page 83).

SERVES: 6

One 3½-pound chicken, cut into serving pieces, or
use 6 chicken pieces (about 3 pounds), with excess fat discarded and skinless if preferred
1 tablespoon red wine vinegar ◆ 6 tablespoons extra-virgin olive oil
1½ tablespoons ground coriander ◆ Coarse sea salt and finely cracked pepper
12 sprigs fresh rosemary or thyme ◆ 3 cups hot chicken broth or water
1½ cups hilopites or orzo

◆

1 Heat the oven to 375°F.

2 By hand, rub the chicken pieces with the vinegar, 2 tablespoons of the olive oil, coriander, salt, and pepper. Arrange in a deep, heavy baking dish or roasting pan, adding 2 tablespoons olive oil and 6 rosemary sprigs to the dish. Bake 20 minutes, turning the pieces once.

3 In a small bowl, combine the remaining olive oil and half the broth (or water); pour into the baking dish. Reduce the oven temperature to 350°F and bake uncovered for 15 minutes; baste once or twice.

4 Remove the dish from the oven, pour in the remaining broth (or water), add the pasta, and salt and pepper to taste.

5 Continue baking 25 to 30 minutes longer or until the sauce has been absorbed by the pasta; gently stir once or twice. (If the dish appears to be browning too quickly, lightly cover with aluminum foil.)

6 Discard the rosemary sprigs and check the seasonings. Transfer chicken and pasta to a platter and garnish with the remaining rosemary sprigs.

Lamb and Orzo Bake

Arni Yiouvetsi

This dish is named for the huge round pot in which it is made, a yiouvetsi. In my village, we take the yiouvetsi to the baker to be cooked. It can be made very successfully in a home oven, but to us, it always tastes better if the baker cooks it!

SERVES: 6

6 small lamb shanks or 3 large lamb shanks, cut crosswise in half by the butcher
6 tablespoons extra-virgin olive oil ◆ 1 tablespoon ground coriander
2 tablespoons dried Greek oregano ◆ Coarse sea salt and finely cracked pepper
6 large, ripe tomatoes, peeled and diced (reserve juices)
1 tablespoon tomato paste mixed with 2 tablespoons water ◆ 4 bay leaves
1 tablespoon allspice ◆ 2½ cups hot lamb or chicken broth, or water ◆ 1½ cups orzo
4 tablespoons chopped fresh flat-leaf parsley
1 cup finely grated kephalotyri, kasseri, or parmesan cheese

◆

1 Heat the oven to 425°F.

2 Trim the lamb shanks of excess fat, rinse well to remove any bone splinters, and arrange in a deep, heavy baking dish or roasting pan. Rub with 4 tablespoons of olive oil, coriander, oregano, salt, and pepper. Bake 20 minutes, turning shanks once.

3 Add the tomatoes and their juices, tomato paste, bay leaves, allspice, remaining olive oil, and half the broth (or water) to the dish. Lower the oven temperature to 350°F, and bake uncovered for 30 minutes; baste once or twice.

4 Remove the dish from the oven and turn the shanks. Pour the remaining broth (or water) into the dish and stir in the pasta. Add salt and pepper to taste. Stirring the pasta once, continue baking another 30 minutes or until all the sauce has been absorbed by the pasta. (If the dish appears to be browning too quickly, lightly cover with aluminum foil.)

5 Check the seasonings, sprinkle with parsley, and serve from the dish. Serve the cheese separately.

Savory Meat and Pasta Pie
Pastitsio

*Pastitsio is always a favorite dish when the family gathers together.
It appears complicated because of its long list of ingredients, but it's not.
It does take a little time to prepare though, so I often make it a day ahead.
Serve with a huge green salad or plates of horta.*

SERVES: 10 to 12

MEAT SAUCE

5 tablespoons extra-virgin olive oil ◆ 2 large onions, finely chopped

1 celery stalk, strings removed, very finely chopped

2 pounds lean lamb or beef, or a mixture, finely ground

1 cup dry red wine ◆ 5 large, ripe tomatoes, peeled and diced (reserve juices)

1 teaspoon sugar ◆ 1 tablespoon tomato paste mixed with 2 tablespoons water

Small bunch of fresh flat-leaf parsley, leaves finely chopped

½ cup meat broth or water ◆ 3 tablespoons dried Greek oregano

1 tablespoon ground cinnamon ◆ 1 teaspoon grated nutmeg

Fine sea salt and finely cracked pepper

9 cups short-tube pasta such as ziti or rigatoni

WHITE SAUCE

4 tablespoons unsalted butter ◆ 4 tablespoons all-purpose flour

2 cups milk, heated to very warm ◆ 3 large eggs, beaten

¾ cup cottage cheese, drained and pressed through a strainer

Fine sea salt and finely cracked pepper

4 tablespoons unsalted butter, melted ◆ 1 cup fresh bread crumbs

½ cup grated aged graviera, kephalotyri, or parmesan cheese

1 Heat the oven to 350°F.

2 Make the meat sauce. Heat the olive oil in a large skillet or sauté pan and sauté the onion and celery over low-medium heat until soft, about 6 minutes. Raise the heat, add the meat, and sauté until lightly browned, breaking up any lumps with a wooden spoon, and stirring occasionally to prevent sticking. Add the wine, and boil until evaporated, about 3 minutes. Add the tomatoes and their juices, the sugar, and the tomato paste. Lower the heat and simmer 10 minutes. Stir in the parsley, broth (or water), oregano, cinnamon, nutmeg, and salt and pepper to taste. Simmer uncovered for 40 minutes or until almost all the liquid has evaporated. Check the seasonings (the sauce should be highly flavored). Remove from the heat and set aside for 10 minutes to cool a little. Cover, and set aside (or refrigerate overnight).

3 Prepare the pasta. Three-quarters fill a large saucepan with water and bring to a boil. Add the pasta, cover the pan, and simmer 8 minutes or until just beginning to soften. Drain, and set aside to cool.

4 Make the white sauce. Set a medium, heavy saucepan over low heat and add the 4 tablespoons butter. When melted, add the flour and cook for 1 minute, stirring constantly with a wooden spoon. Gradually add the milk, about a ¼ cup at a time, stirring constantly. Bring to a boil, still stirring, and remove the pan from the heat. Set aside 10 minutes to cool slightly.

5 Beat in the eggs, stir in the cottage cheese, and season with salt and pepper.

6 In a large bowl, combine the pasta with half the white sauce.

7 Choose a heavy, rectangular (approximately 9 by 12 inches) or round (10-inch diameter) baking dish, and brush with half the melted butter. Spread one-third of the pasta mixture in the dish, and cover with half the meat sauce. Gently spread another one-third of the pasta over the meat, cover with the remaining meat sauce, and finish with the last one-third of pasta. Pour over the remaining white sauce and lightly smooth the top with a spatula. Sprinkle the bread crumbs and graviera cheese on top, and drizzle on the rest of the melted butter.

8 Bake uncovered for 50 minutes or until the top is browned. Let the pie rest for 15 minutes before cutting into serving portions.

Pasta with Wild Greens and Olive Oil
Macaronia me Horta

Quick, inexpensive, and very easy to prepare, macaronia me horta is a good dish to have in your repertoire. Serve with slices of graviera or kephalotyri cheese.

SERVES: 4

**Large handful of young beet greens or mustard greens,
or a mixture of young spinach and chard** ◆ **6 tablespoons extra-virgin olive oil
6 green onions, including unblemished green parts,
trimmed and cut into thin diagonal slivers** ◆ **Small handful of fresh flat-leaf parsley, leaves
coarsely chopped** ◆ **Freshly squeezed lemon juice to taste
6 cups elbow pasta, or other short-tube pasta such as rigatoni
Coarse sea salt and finely cracked pepper to taste**

◆

1 Strip the leaves from any tough stems and wash well; shake off excess water. Discard the thick or tough stems, and cut the slender stems into thin, 1-inch lengths. Tear the leaves into large pieces.

2 Half fill a large saucepan with water and bring to a boil. Add the pasta and simmer until just tender; drain.

3 Meanwhile, set a heavy sauté pan or skillet over low heat and add 3 tablespoons of the olive oil. When warm, add any stems from the greens and the green onions, and cook 2 minutes. Add the greens and parsley, and cook until wilted, about 4 minutes; stir once or twice with a wooden spoon. Sprinkle with lemon juice, and add the pasta and remaining olive oil. Cook 1 minute longer, shaking the pan once or twice, to mix everything together.

4 Season the dish generously with salt and pepper, and divide between warm bowls.

Macaroni with Herbs and Cheese
Macaronia me Votana ke Tyri

*Served alone, macaronia makes a substantial and attractive lunch or supper dish.
It can also be served as a delicious side dish, and it's my favorite accompaniment to
Veal Pot Roast (see page 59) and Roast Quail in Grape Leaves (see page 50).
The secret to its fine flavor is the good broth, a generous quantity of cheese,
and plenty of fresh herbs.*

SERVES: 6

**2 cups good-quality chicken or meat broth
4½ cups "elbow" pasta (macaroni) ◆ ½ cup extra-virgin olive oil
6 green onions, including unblemished green parts, finely sliced
Small handful of mixed fresh herb leaves such as thyme, marjoram, fennel, borage,
sorrel, savory, and chervil, snipped or finely chopped
Small handful of fresh flat-leaf parsley, leaves coarsely chopped
1 tablespoon dried Greek oregano, crumbled ◆ Juice of 1 small lemon or to taste
Coarse sea salt and finely cracked pepper to taste
¾ cup finely grated aged myzithra or kasseri cheese**

1 Bring the broth and 2 cups water to a boil in a large saucepan. Add the pasta, bring back to a boil, cover the pan, and simmer until just cooked, about 10 minutes. Drain, and rinse out the saucepan.

2 Return the saucepan to low heat and add the olive oil. Add the green onions and cook 2 minutes or until softened. Add the herbs, parsley, and oregano, and warm through. Add half the lemon juice and the pasta, stir to mix, and heat to warm.

3 Transfer to a warm serving bowl and sprinkle with lemon juice to taste, salt, pepper, and the cheese. Serve immediately.

Roasted Vegetable Pilaf
Pilafi Lakhanika

When you are using your oven to bake something else, roast a tray of vegetables (eggplants, zucchini, onions, tomatoes, peppers, or a mixture) at the same time. The next day, make this pilafi. During the summer, when we have our second longest fast (we have a lot of fasts!), this makes an excellent lunch when served with Chickpea and Sesame Dip (see page 12), or serve with it sausages or cheese.

SERVES: 6 to 8

2 medium eggplants, trimmed, cut lengthwise in half, then crosswise in three pieces
2 medium bell peppers, any color, cut into quarters or 6 pieces,
with seeds and seed boxes discarded ◆ 6 small onions
3 medium zucchini, trimmed, cut lengthwise in half, then crosswise in half
10 tablespoons extra-virgin olive oil ◆ 4 plump cloves garlic
2 tablespoons dried Greek oregano ◆ Coarse sea salt and finely cracked pepper to taste
1 cup long-grained white rice such as Carolina or Patna ◆ 3 bay leaves
3 cups light chicken or meat broth, or water ◆ 12 small tomatoes
1 tablespoon red wine vinegar ◆ ½ teaspoon sugar
4 tablespoons finely chopped fresh flat-leaf parsley or mixed fresh herbs such as dill,
fennel, marjoram, or thyme ◆ Pinch of paprika ◆ Lemon wedges

◆

1 Heat the oven to 350°F.

2 Arrange the eggplants, peppers, onions, and zucchini in a large baking dish. Pour over 5 tablespoons of the olive oil, and push the garlic cloves down between the vegetables. Sprinkle everything with oregano, a little salt and, more generously, with pepper.

Add ½ cup water to the dish. Bake uncovered for 40 minutes or until the vegetables are cooked and well browned; turn once or twice in the dish, and baste.

3 Meanwhile, cook the rice. Set a heavy saucepan over low heat and add 2 tablespoons olive oil. Add the rice, and stir with a wooden spoon until

the grains whiten, about 2 minutes. Add the bay leaves, salt, and broth (or water). Raise the heat to low-medium and boil uncovered, without stirring, until the liquid has disappeared and holes appear in the surface of the rice, about 10 minutes. Remove from the heat, cover the pan with a clean kitchen towel or 2 layers of paper towels and a tight-fitting lid, and set aside in a warm spot (but not over direct heat).

4 Twenty minutes before the vegetables are cooked, arrange the tomatoes in a heavy baking dish just large enough to hold them in a single layer. Sprinkle with the remaining 3 tablespoons olive oil, the vinegar, and the sugar, and add a few tablespoons water to the dish. Bake uncovered 15 to 20 minutes or until well browned.

5 Transfer the rice to a large, warm platter or shallow bowl, and lightly separate the grains with a fork. Surround with the vegetables. Sprinkle the pilaf with parsley, paprika, salt, pepper, and the pan juices from the vegetables and tomatoes. Serve hot, warm, or at room temperature, with lemon wedges.

Carrot and Pine Nut Pilaf
Karrota Pilafi

Make this pretty little dish when you have young, sweet carrots and some cilantro.
It's very good hot or cold, and it can be served alone or with horta
or a purslane or arugula salad.

SERVES: 6

14 small, young, sweet carrots or 6 medium carrots
¼ cup extra-virgin olive oil ◆ 1 teaspoon ground coriander
4 bay leaves ◆ ½ cup long-grained white rice such as Carolina or Patna
Coarse sea salt to taste ◆ ½ cup pine nuts, lightly toasted
4 tablespoons chopped cilantro ◆ 1 small red onion, quartered and thinly sliced
Juice of ½ small lemon ◆ Finely cracked pepper to taste

◆

1 Scrape the carrots, rinse, and cut lengthwise in half (or peel larger carrots and julienne).

2 Set a large, heavy saucepan or casserole over low heat and add the olive oil. Add the carrots, ground coriander, and bay leaves, and stir with a wooden spoon or fork to coat the carrots. Sprinkle over the rice and a little salt, gently shake the pan to mix everything together, and add water to barely cover the carrots. Simmer uncovered for 20 to 30 minutes or until the carrots and rice are cooked but still appear to be a little moist.

3 Turn out the pilaf onto a platter. Scatter over the pine nuts, cilantro, and onion, and sprinkle with lemon juice, salt, and pepper.

Spinach Rice
Spanakorizo

At certain times of the year, the spinach in my garden has a better, more distinctively spinach flavor than it does at other times. This is the spinach I like to use to make spanakorizo. Serve as a simple lunch or supper dish with olives and slices of feta cheese, or as a side dish to grilled meats.

SERVES: 6

2 medium leeks ◆ 6 tablespoons extra-virgin olive oil or to taste
6 green onions, including unblemished green parts, trimmed and cut into diagonal slivers
1 plump clove garlic, finely chopped ◆ 6 sprigs of fresh dill, chopped
1 tablespoon dried Greek oregano
2 pounds fresh spinach, rinsed and leaves stripped from tough stems
½ cup long-grain white rice such as Carolina or Patna
Coarse sea salt and finely cracked pepper ◆ Lemon wedges

◆

1. Slice off the roots and green tops from the leeks. Cut a vertical slit in each one, through to the center. Holding upright under running water, gently pull the layers apart, one at a time, to wash out any grit or dirt; shake off the excess water. Thinly slice the leeks.

2. Set a large, heavy saucepan or casserole over low heat and add 3 tablespoons of the olive oil. Add the leeks and sauté, stirring occasionally, until soft (about 5 minutes). Add the green onions and garlic, stir to mix, and cook 1 minute longer. Add the dill and oregano and cook 1 minute or until the dill wilts.

3. Slice the spinach leaves into 1-inch ribbons and add to the pan. Stir until wilted, about 2 minutes. Add the remaining olive oil, the rice, salt, pepper, and enough water to cover by 1 inch. Raise the heat to low-medium and boil uncovered about 10 minutes, until the liquid disappears and holes appear in the surface of the rice. Remove from the heat, cover the pan with a clean kitchen towel or 2 layers of paper towels and a tight-fitting lid, and set aside 30 minutes.

4. At serving time, return the pan to very low heat for 1 minute. Check the seasonings. Serve on a warm platter or from the pan, with lemon wedges.

chapter six

BREADS
& SAVORY PIES

Family Bread
Khoriatiko Psomi

This is the bread I like to make most days of the week. Barley flour, olive oil, and honey provide the bread with an excellent flavor and firm crumb, and its chewy, dense texture is perfectly suited to making Rusks (see page 111).

MAKES: 2 loaves

1 cup water, heated to tepid (110°F) ♦ 2 tablespoons active dry yeast
2 tablespoons honey ♦ 2 teaspoons fine sea salt
1 large egg, lightly beaten ♦ ¾ cup milk, heated to tepid (110°F)
2 tablespoons extra-virgin olive oil ♦ 2 tablespoons unsalted butter, melted
2¼ cups barley flour ♦ 2½ to 2¾ cups strong bread flour

♦

1 Pour ¼ cup of the tepid water into a small bowl and sprinkle over the yeast; set aside in a warm spot for 10 minutes or until foamy.

2 In a medium bowl, combine the honey, salt, egg, milk, remaining tepid water, 1 tablespoon of the olive oil, and 1 tablespoon butter.

3 Sift the barley flour and half the bread flour into a large mixing bowl. Make a well in the center and pour in the yeast and honey mixtures; stir to mix. Knead for 10 minutes, gradually adding enough of the remaining flour to make a firm, smooth, and elastic dough. Tightly cover the bowl, and set aside in a warm draft-free spot for 1½ hours or until the dough has doubled in bulk.

4 Brush a baking tray with a little of the remaining olive oil. Knead the dough 1 minute. Form into 2 round loaves and place well apart on the baking tray. Cover with a clean kitchen towel and set aside to rise in a warm spot for 1 hour.

5 Heat the oven to 375°F.

6 Combine the butter and remaining olive oil and brush the loaves. Bake 40 minutes or until the loaves are lightly browned and sound hollow when tapped on the bottom. Cool on a rack.

Rusks
Paximathi

Bread becomes stale very quickly in our hot climate. To ensure we always have a supply of bread for our tables, we turn some of our fresh-baked bread into paximathi—hard, dry bread that we can store for months, if necessary. When we want to use it, we soak the dried bread in water and olive oil. As if by magic, it springs back to life. To make successful paximathi, you need good-quality, densely textured bread (see page 110). I like to serve paximathi for lunch, with a creamy cheese dip and green olives.

SERVES: 6

1 loaf Family Bread (page 110), halved horizontally ◆ ½ cup water
1 cup extra-virgin olive oil ◆ 18 ripe cherry or tiny tomatoes
Coarse sea salt and finely cracked pepper to taste
⅔ cup feta cheese, drained and crumbled
⅔ cup cottage cheese, drained and pressed through a strainer
½ cup strained yogurt ◆ 2 tablespoons finely chopped fresh flat-leaf parsley
2 tablespoons dried Greek oregano, crumbled

◆

1 To make the paximathi: Heat the oven to 225°F. Lay the bread, cut sides up, on a baking tray. Bake 50 minutes or until hard, turning once; cool on a rack. Store one half-loaf for another occasion.

2 To revive the paximathi: Break the bread into pieces over a bowl. Sprinkle with the water and 3 tablespoons of the olive oil; set aside 30 minutes.

3 Cut the tomatoes in half, sprinkle with salt and pepper, and add to the bread.

4 In a medium bowl, combine the feta cheese, cottage cheese, yogurt, and 3 tablespoons olive oil. Stir to mix with a wooden spoon.

5 Arrange the bread and tomatoes on one side of a platter and sprinkle with parsley and the remaining olive oil. Scoop the cheese mixture onto the other side of the platter and sprinkle with oregano.

Olive Bread Rolls

Eliopsomo

*Rolls are very useful to have on hand—they are easy to carry and stay fresh longer
than a cut loaf of bread. Olive bread, especially, keeps very well,
and it has a very satisfying flavor.*

MAKES: 10 rolls

1 teaspoon honey ◆ 1 cup water, heated to tepid (110°F) ◆ 1½ tablespoons active dry yeast
½ cup extra-virgin olive oil ◆ 2 teaspoons fine sea salt ◆ 2¼ to 3¼ cups whole-wheat flour
2¼ to 3¼ cups strong bread flour
1 large onion, finely chopped ◆ 14 plump Greek olives such as Amfissa or Thasos,
drained and pitted ◆ 1 tablespoon dried Greek oregano, crumbled

1 In a small bowl, combine the honey and water, and sprinkle over the yeast. Set aside in a warm place until foamy, about 10 minutes. Whisk in 3 tablespoons of the olive oil and the salt.

2 Sift half the whole-wheat flour and half the bread flour into a large mixing bowl. Make a well in the center and pour in the yeast mixture; stir to mix. Knead 10 minutes, gradually adding enough of the remaining flour to make a firm, smooth, and elastic dough. Tightly cover the bowl and set aside in a warm, draft-free spot for 2 hours or until the dough has doubled in bulk.

3 Set a heavy skillet over low heat and add 3 tablespoons olive oil. Add the onion and sauté until very soft, about 10 minutes. Set aside.

4 Half fill a small saucepan of water and bring to a boil. Add the olives, drain, and pat dry on paper towels. Coarsely chop half the olives, and finely chop the rest. Add all the olives and oregano to the onion and mix, then add to the dough and knead 1 minute.

5 Brush a heavy baking tray with olive oil. Form the dough into 10 rolls and arrange on the tray, spaced well apart. Cover with a kitchen towel and set aside to rise 1 hour in a warm draft-free spot.

6 Heat the oven to 375°F. Bake 10 minutes, then brush the rolls with the remaining olive oil. Lower the oven temperature to 350°F and bake 20 to 25 minutes longer, or until deep golden brown and rolls sound hollow when tapped on the bottom.

Chicken and Spinach Pie

Kotopitta me Spanaki

Perfect for picnics, I make this pie when we spend the day at the beach or in the mountains. I like to use phyllo when I want to make kotopitta quickly, but I sometimes make it with the same pie dough that I use for Fennel Pies (see page 118–119).

SERVES: 8 to 10

FILLING

1½ pounds fresh spinach, leaves stripped from stems ◆ ½ cup extra-virgin olive oil

8 green onions, including unblemished green parts, trimmed and thinly sliced

6 sprigs of fresh dill, coarsely chopped ◆ ½ teaspoon grated nutmeg

Small bunch of fresh flat-leaf parsley, leaves coarsely chopped

Finely cracked pepper to taste

¾ cup cottage cheese, drained and pressed through a fine strainer

⅔ cup feta cheese, drained and crumbled ◆ 3 large eggs, beaten

1½ pounds cooked chicken, without skin or bones, cut into small bite-sized pieces

Fine sea salt ◆ One 1-pound package phyllo, thawed if frozen

4 tablespoons unsalted butter, melted

◆

1 Heat the oven to 350°F.

2 Rinse the spinach in several changes of cold water and discard any bruised or tough leaves. Set a large, heavy saucepan over low heat and add the spinach. Cover, and cook with just the water on the leaves for 1 minute or until the leaves start to wilt. Drain, pressing the greens against the sides of the colander to remove as much liquid as possible. Transfer to a cutting board. With a large knife, coarsely chop, and set aside.

3 Set a heavy sauté pan or skillet over low heat and add the olive oil. Add the green onions and sauté over low heat until soft, about 2 minutes. With a wooden spoon, stir in the dill, spinach, nutmeg, half the parsley, and pepper, and cook 1 minute. Remove from the heat and set aside.

4 In a large bowl, combine the cottage cheese, feta cheese, and eggs. Using a fork, mash together until thoroughly mixed. Add the chicken pieces, the remaining parsley, and salt to taste (feta cheese can be salty). Stir to mix.

5 Remove the phyllo from the refrigerator, and set aside. In a small bowl, combine the melted butter with the remaining olive oil. Divide the phyllo into 2 portions; wrap 1 portion in plastic wrap and refrigerate.

6 Make the pie: Choose a 10-inch square or round baking pan, at least 2 inches deep, and brush with the oil/butter mixture. Line with 1 phyllo sheet, gently pressing it against the sides of the pan, and brush with the oil/butter. Repeat with the remaining unrefrigerated phyllo, but don't brush the last sheet. Turn a round pan 60 degrees each time you add 1 sheet, a square pan 90 degrees.

7 With a spatula, lightly spread the chicken mixture over the phyllo and evenly spread the spinach mixture on top, separating the greens with a fork as you work. Fold the edges of the phyllo over the filling, and brush with the oil/butter. Remove the second portion of phyllo from the refrigerator. Lay 1 sheet over the filling, letting the edges hang over the sides of the pan. Lightly brush with the oil/butter mixture, and layer until all the sheets are used; don't brush the last sheet.

8 Carefully ease your fingers down between the edge of the pie and the sides of the pan, pull the bottom edges of the pie toward the center, and tuck the top sheets in around the bottom of the pie. Liberally brush the top sheet with the remaining oil/butter mixture. With a small, sharp knife, score the top 2 sheets of phyllo in a square baking pan into squares or diamond shapes, for serving. (Don't score a round pie—it would be impossible to remove it from the pan later.) Bake 45 to 50 minutes or until deep golden brown.

9 Remove the pie from the oven and immediately cut through the score marks of a square pie, to the bottom of the pan. Serve from the pan or arrange the pieces on a dish. To transfer a round pie to a serving platter, invert a large plate over the baking pan. Holding the plate firmly in place, turn pan and plate upside down. Carefully remove the pan. Invert a serving platter over the bottom of the pie and, firmly holding platter and pie, turn the pie the right side up. Serve hot, warm, or at room temperature.

Leeks, Chard, and Beet Greens Pie
Prassopitta

Whenever I have plenty of vegetables, I make a pie. In the fall and winter, I fill pies with leeks, spinach, chard, beet greens, and wild greens such as dandelion, arugula, mustard, and chickweed. In the summer, my favorite pie filling is a combination of zucchini and green onions. Serve hot, warm, or at room temperature.

SERVES: 8 to 10

FILLING
1½ cups milk ◆ ⅓ cup semolina ◆ ½ teaspoon finely grated nutmeg ◆ 3 large eggs, beaten
1⅓ cups feta cheese, drained and finely grated ◆ ½ cup extra-virgin olive oil
3 medium leeks, washed, trimmed of most of the green, and thinly sliced
6 green onions, including unblemished green parts, trimmed and thinly sliced
Small handful of fresh dill or flat-leaf parsley, leaves coarsely chopped
4 packed cups chard (about 1 pound), leaves stripped from tough stems
Large handful of beet greens, leaves stripped from tough stems
Fine sea salt and finely cracked pepper to taste

PIE
One 1-pound package phyllo, thawed if frozen ◆ 4 tablespoons unsalted butter, melted
¾ cup cottage cheese, drained and pressed through a fine strainer

◆

1 Heat the oven to 350°F.

2 Make the filling. Pour the milk into a small heavy saucepan over low heat. When warm, whisk in the semolina. Slowly bring to a boil, stirring with a wooden spoon. Add the nutmeg and whisk in the eggs. Remove pan from the heat and set aside to cool a little. Stir in the feta cheese.

3 Set a large, heavy sauté pan or skillet over low heat and add half the olive oil. Add the leeks and stir occasionally until just soft, about 8 minutes. Stir in the green onions and dill (or parsley), cook 1 minute longer, and set aside.

4 Thoroughly wash the chard and beet greens under cold water. Strip the greens from any tender stems; coarsely chop the stems and tear greens into large pieces.

5 Pour 2 inches water into a large saucepan and bring to a boil. Add the stems and cook 1 minute; drain. Return the empty pan to low heat and add the greens (with only the water clinging to the leaves). Cover, and cook for 1 minute or until the leaves start to wilt. Drain in a colander, pressing the greens against the sides to remove as much liquid as possible.

6 Add the semolina cheese mixture to the leeks, and season with salt and pepper; briefly mix.

7 Remove the phyllo from the refrigerator and set aside. In a small bowl, combine the melted butter with the remaining olive oil. Divide the phyllo into 2 portions; wrap 1 portion in plastic wrap and refrigerate.

8 Make the pie. Choose a 10-inch square or round baking pan, at least 2 inches deep, and brush with the oil/butter mixture. Line with 1 phyllo sheet, gently pressing it against the sides of the pan, and brush with the oil/butter. Repeat with the remaining unrefrigerated phyllo, but don't brush the last sheet. Turn a round pan 60 degrees each time you add 1 sheet, a square pan 90 degrees. With a spatula, lightly spread the leek/semolina mixture over the phyllo.

Evenly spread the greens on top, separating them with a fork as you work, and spoon the cottage cheese over the greens.

9 Sprinkle with pepper, and salt if desired (feta cheese can be salty).

10 Fold the edges of the phyllo over the filling, and brush with the oil/butter.

11 Remove the second portion of phyllo from the refrigerator. Lay 1 sheet over the filling, letting the edges hang over the sides of the pan. Lightly brush with the oil/butter mixture, and layer until all the sheets are used; don't brush the last sheet.

12 Carefully ease your fingers down between the edge of the pie and the sides of the pan, pull the bottom edges of the pie toward the center, and tuck the top sheets in around the bottom of the pie. Liberally brush the top sheet with the remaining oil/butter mixture. With a small, sharp knife, score the top 2 sheets of phyllo in a square baking pan into squares or diamond shapes, for serving. (Don't score a round pie—it would be impossible to remove it from the pan later.)

13 Bake 45 to 50 minutes until golden brown.

14 Remove the pie from the oven and immediately cut through the score marks of a square pie to the bottom of the pan. Serve from the pan, or arrange the pieces on a dish.

Fennel Pies

Marathopittes

*Serve these delicious sesame-topped small pies on a meze table or as a light lunch,
with a salad. Although I make them with pie dough here, you can use phyllo if you
prefer. Fill them with all sorts of other vegetables such as eggplants,
zucchini, or spinach, or even rice.*

MAKES: 12 to 16 pies

PIE DOUGH

2 cups all-purpose flour plus 4 tablespoons ◆ 2 tablespoons chickpea flour
1 teaspoon fine sea salt or to taste ◆ ¼ cup extra-virgin olive oil
1 large egg, separated; white lightly beaten ◆ 3 tablespoons freshly squeezed lemon juice

FILLING

3 tablespoons extra-virgin olive oil
3 medium leeks, washed, trimmed of most of their green, and thinly sliced
Small handful of fresh fennel, coarsely chopped
4 tablespoons chopped fresh flat-leaf parsley ◆ Coarse sea salt and finely cracked pepper
⅔ cup cottage cheese, drained and pressed through a fine strainer
⅓ cup feta cheese, drained and crumbled ◆ ⅓ cup sesame seeds

◆

1 Make the pie dough. In a large bowl, combine the 2 cups all-purpose flour, the chickpea flour, salt, 2 tablespoons olive oil, egg white, and 2 tablespoons lemon juice. Knead to make a smooth and elastic dough, about 5 minutes; add a few drops of water if necessary. Tightly wrap in plastic wrap and refrigerate 1 hour.

2 Make the filling. Pour the olive oil into a large, heavy sauté pan or skillet set over low heat. Add the leeks and sauté until soft, about 12 minutes; stir occasionally. Stir in the fennel, parsley, salt, and pepper, and cook 1 minute. Remove from the heat and pour off any liquid. Add the cottage cheese and feta cheese, and lightly stir to mix.

3 Heat the oven to 350°F. Lightly brush a baking tray with a little of the remaining olive oil.

4 Divide the dough in half, rewrap 1 portion, and return this to the refrigerator. Scatter the remaining 4 tablespoons flour over a clean work surface and roll out the pie dough as thinly as possible. Use a 2-inch round cutter or inverted glass to cut into circles. Place 1 heaped tablespoon of filling in the centers of half the circles. Brush the edges of these circles with the remaining lemon juice and place a second circle on top of each one. Crimp the edges with a fork to seal. Repeat with the remaining pie dough and filling.

5 Arrange the pies 2 inches apart on the baking tray. In a small bowl, whisk together the egg yolk and remaining olive oil and liberally brush the pies with this glaze. Bake 10 minutes. Sprinkle the sesame seeds over the pies and bake 10 minutes longer or until deep golden brown. Serve hot, warm, or at room temperature.

Small Pies of Wild Greens
Hortopittes

My grandmother, who was from Crete, taught me how to make these pies. She had a special knack for finding the most delicious, most tender horta, or wild greens. If you can't find horta in your local markets, substitute beet greens, chard, or spinach. You can make the pies in triangle or rectangle shapes and serve them the way my grandmother did—as a side dish to roast or grilled pork—or as a light lunch, with slices of aged graviera or kephalotyri cheese.

MAKES: 24 to 30 pies

FILLING

3 pounds young vlita (amaranth greens or water spinach), beet greens, or ruby chard

10 tablespoons extra-virgin olive oil, or more as needed

2 medium mild onions, quartered and thinly sliced ◆ 1½ teaspoon ground coriander

½ teaspoon ground cumin ◆ 1 tablespoon dried Greek oregano

Small bunch of fresh dill or fennel, coarsely chopped

Coarse sea salt and finely cracked pepper to taste

Juice of ½ lemon ◆ One 1-pound package phyllo (at least 12 sheets), thawed if frozen

Lemon wedges

◆

1 Heat the oven to 350°F.

2 Rinse the greens in several changes of cold water. Discard the stems and any tough or discolored leaves.

3 Pour ½ inch water into a large saucepan and place over low-medium heat. Bring to a boil, add the greens, and cook for 5 minutes or until barely tender. Drain in a colander, pressing firmly against the sides to remove as much water as possible; blot with paper towels. Transfer to a cutting board and finely chop.

4 Set a heavy sauté pan or skillet over low heat and add 5 tablespoons of the olive oil. Add the onion and sauté until soft, about 10 minutes. Stir in the coriander, cumin, and oregano. Add

the greens and dill (or fennel) and cook 2 minutes. Add salt, pepper, and lemon juice.

5 Brush 2 baking trays with a little of the remaining olive oil. Divide the phyllo into 2 portions. Wrap 1 portion in plastic wrap and refrigerate. Divide the remaining sheets in half; fold 1 portion in half and loosely cover with plastic wrap. Set aside. Lay the remaining sheets, stacked on top of each other, on the table, with the shorter side facing you.

6 To make triangles: Cut the phyllo sheets lengthwise into 3 strips and stack the strips on top of each other. Remove the top strip from the pile and lightly brush with olive oil. Place a second strip on top of the first, and lightly brush that one too.

7 Place 2 tablespoons of the greens mixture on the bottom end of the oiled strips. Take the bottom right corner of both strips between finger and thumb and fold over to the left side to make a triangle. Gently pull up the bottom left corner

and fold up to make a second triangle. Continue folding until you reach the top. Place seam side down on the baking tray, spaced 1 inch apart. Repeat with all the remaining phyllo and greens.

8 To make rolls: Cut the phyllo sheets lengthwise into 2 strips and stack on top of each other. Remove the top strip from the pile and lightly brush with olive oil. Place a second strip on top of the first, and lightly brush that one. Spread 2 tablespoons of the greens mixture along the bottom of the strip, leaving a ¾-inch border along the lower edge and the sides. Fold the lower edges of the strips over the greens and roll over twice. Bring both sides over the greens, lightly brush with olive oil, and roll up the strip. Place seam side down on the baking tray, spaced 1 inch apart. Repeat with all remaining phyllo and greens.

9 Brush the pies with the remaining olive oil and bake 20 to 25 minutes or until crisp and golden. Serve with lemon wedges.

Mama says...
You can freeze these pies too: Make the pies as described, but don't bake them. Spread the uncooked pies in a single layer on a baking tray and freeze. Transfer to freezer bags, and store in the freezer for up to 2 months. Defrost before baking.

chapter seven

DESSERTS
& SWEET THINGS

Honey-Baked Figs
Sika sto Fourno

My fig trees produce hundreds of figs every year. As well as making jam with them, I follow Greek tradition and dry them. We lay sacking over the roof, and spread the figs on it to dry out in the sun. Then we thread the figs on long, thin reeds collected from the river nearby. I put bay leaves between the figs, as insects don't seem to like their smell, and hang the strings over the rafters of our storehouse. For the rest of the year we have deliciously sweet figs for mezes, breads, cakes, and puddings. We also enjoy these luscious, ripe fruits just as they are, but when we have fallen figs that are not quite ripe, or still firm, we turn them into this syrupy-sweet bake. Serve with slices of myzithra or manouri cheese or with strained yogurt.

SERVES: 6

12 large or 18 medium firm, fresh figs
4 tablespoons Hymettus or other strongly flavored honey
½ cup Mavrodaphne or Samos wine, or water
1 to 2 teaspoons rose water to taste (optional)

◆

1 Heat the oven to 325°F.

2 Rinse the figs and trim the stems. Arrange in a single layer, stem ends up, in a heavy baking dish just large enough to hold them.

3 In a small bowl, combine the honey and wine and pour over the figs. Add enough water to cover the bottom of the dish. Bake uncovered for 15 minutes; baste once or twice with the syrup. Bake small figs 15 minutes longer, medium figs 25 minutes longer; baste occasionally and add a few tablespoons of water if necessary to prevent the syrup from scorching.

4 Transfer the figs to a platter, spoon over the syrup, and sprinkle with rose water.

Quinces in Wine Syrup
Kydonia Glykisma

*Quinces are quite difficult to peel, which can mean a lot of work for the cook.
But I love their powerful aroma so much that I make this pretty dish as often as
I can. Serve with slices of aged graviera or kephalotyri cheese, or with
Little Rice Puddings (see page 133).*

SERVES: 6

2 cups dry red wine ◆ ½ cup Hymettus or other strongly flavored honey
4 medium quinces ◆ 4 cloves
½ cup unsalted pistachios, coarsely chopped or 3 tablespoons flaked almonds, lightly toasted
Large pinch of freshly grated nutmeg (optional)

◆

1 Place a medium, nonreactive saucepan over low heat, add the wine and honey, and slowly bring to a boil.

2 Using a stiff brush, scrub the quinces under running water to remove the soft fuzz on their skins. Cut lengthwise into six or eight pieces, and core. Add to the pan with the cloves. Cover, bring back to a low boil, and simmer 1 hour or until the quinces are soft.

3 With a slotted spoon, transfer the quinces from the pan to a bowl; set aside.

4 Raise the heat and boil the syrup uncovered until reduced to about 1½ cups. Remove the cloves and discard.

5 Peel the quinces and arrange in a shallow serving dish. Pour over the syrup and set aside to cool to room temperature. To serve, sprinkle with pistachios (or almonds) and nutmeg.

Apricot Pudding
Verikokko Glykismo

In early summer, we have a glorious abundance of apricots. The problem is that there are far too many for me to use in the short time that the fruits are ripe. For this reason, I dry most of them to use later in the year for desserts such as this one. This recipe can also be made using prunes, dried figs, or fresh apple or pear slices instead of apricots.

SERVES: 6

1 cup dried apricots, quartered ◆ Juice of 1 large orange
4 tablespoons pudding rice or short-grained white rice
1½ cups whole milk ◆ Pinch of salt to taste
1½ tablespoons vanilla sugar or 1½ tablespoons sugar plus ¼ teaspoon vanilla extract
4 tablespoons unsalted butter ◆ 6 tablespoons Hymettus or other strongly flavored honey
3 large eggs, separated ◆ ½ cup light cream
1 tablespoon orange flower water (optional)

◆

1 In a small bowl, combine the apricots and orange juice and set aside 2 hours.

2 Heat the oven to 325°F, and arrange a shelf in the middle.

3 Blanch the rice. Pour 2 inches water into a small saucepan and bring to a boil. Stir in the rice and immediately remove the pan from the heat; drain.

4 Set a medium, heavy saucepan over low heat and add the milk. When warm, add the rice and salt. Stirring occasionally with a wooden spoon, simmer 15 to 20 minutes or until the mixture is smooth and creamy but still quite moist. Stir in the vanilla sugar (or sugar and vanilla extract) and 3 tablespoons butter.

5 Butter a 7-inch soufflé dish or deep cake pan with the remaining 1 tablespoon butter. Add the

honey, and tilt the dish to distribute evenly. (If the honey is very thick, place the dish over very low heat for 1 minute or until the honey thins and covers the bottom of the dish.)

6 In a small bowl, beat the egg yolks until pale and frothy. Stir into the rice with the cream, the apricots, and their orange juice marinade.

7 Using a large whisk or electric mixer, whisk the egg whites until stiff. With a metal spoon, stir one-third into the rice mixture, then lightly fold in the remainder. Pour the mixture into the dish and place on the middle shelf of the oven. Bake 45 minutes or until the pudding is set. Let cool to warm or room temperature.

8 Run a palette knife between the pudding and the sides of the dish, to loosen the pudding. Invert a serving plate over the dish and, firmly holding both the dish and plate, turn upside down. Sprinkle with the orange flower water, if desired.

Apple Fritters

Mila

These fritters are very simple to make, and I think you will find that they are very popular. They may be prepared using a deep-fat fryer, if you prefer.

SERVES: 6

Safflower oil, or other oil suitable for frying ◆ 2 eggs, separated
¾ cup all-purpose flour ◆ ¼ teaspoon powdered ginger or ½ teaspoon ground cinnamon
2 tablespoons currants ◆ 1 tablespoon Hymettus or other strongly flavored honey
3 crisp apples ◆ Superfine sugar

◆

1 Pour a 1-inch layer oil into a heavy sauté pan. Place over low heat and bring slowly to a very hot (but not smoking) temperature.

2 In a large bowl, whisk the egg yolks until frothy. Sift in the flour and ginger (or cinnamon) and stir well.

3 In a small bowl, combine the currants and honey; add to the flour batter.

4 Peel the apples. Grate or very thinly slice, and stir into the batter with a wooden spoon.

5 In a large clean bowl, whisk the egg whites until thick, but not stiff. Fold into the batter.

6 Test the heat of the oil by dropping in a small quantity of batter—if it sizzles, the oil is ready. Drop spoonfuls of the batter into the oil, and fry the fritters until golden brown. Don't overcrowd the pan; if necessary, fry in several batches. Using a slotted spoon, transfer the fritters to paper towels to drain. Keep warm while you fry all the fritters. Dust with sugar and serve immediately.

Mama says...
I sometimes make these fritters with pears or fresh apricots instead of apples. Cherries are the best substitute of all though, but be sure to pit them first!

Semolina Honey Pudding

Halvas

We Greeks sometimes have a very sweet tooth. Although we often prefer fresh fruit at the end of a meal, we do like to have little mouthfuls of something very sweet—sometimes several times a day! A visit from a friend or relative is just the excuse I need to produce these sweet treats.

MAKES: 8 servings

¾ cup Hymettus or other strongly flavored honey ◆ ½ cup superfine sugar
4 tablespoons butter ◆ ½ cup fine-grain semolina ◆ ½ teaspoon ground cinnamon
½ cup freshly squeezed orange juice
4 tablespoons chopped unsalted pistachio nuts

◆

1 Place a medium, heavy saucepan over low heat and add the honey, sugar, and butter. Stir with a wooden spoon until the sugar has melted, about 4 minutes; don't let it boil.

2 Add the semolina, cinnamon, and orange juice; stir to mix. Stirring frequently, continue cooking until the mixture is a deep gold and stiff enough to hold its shape, 10 to 15 minutes.

3 Either transfer the halvas to a shallow dish, large enough to hold it in a 1-inch layer or divide between small serving dishes or paper cups set on a tray. Smooth the top (or tops) with a spatula and sprinkle the pistachios over. Cover with a clean kitchen towel, set aside to cool, then refrigerate until cold.

4 To serve the large halvas, cut into pieces.

Vanilla Custard Pies
Galaktoboureka

The cheese in these pies prevents them from being overwhelmingly sweet and satisfies my natural desire to provide nutritious food for my family. Galaktoboureka are easy to make and perfect for entertaining, as they require no last-minute work. I shape them into rectangles in this recipe, but you can also shape the pies into triangles, squares, or cigars. They become gooey and mellow if left in the syrup overnight, but they taste so good when they are warm and fresh that I doubt you will ever have any left to taste in their true, sticky glory.

MAKES: 16 to 24 small pies (depending on the number of phyllo sheets in the package)

FILLING

2½ cups whole milk ◆ 3 large eggs, separated
½ cup vanilla sugar or ½ cup superfine sugar plus ½ teaspoon vanilla extract
½ cup fine-grain semolina ◆ 1 tablespoon unsalted butter
1 cup cottage cheese, drained and pressed through a strainer
⅓ cup feta cheese, drained and finely grated

SYRUP

1 cup Hymettus or other strongly flavored honey ◆ 1 cup superfine sugar
1 cup water ◆ Zest and juice of 1 small organic lemon
One 3-inch cinnamon stick, broken into 2 pieces
2 tablespoons rose water or to taste ◆ ¾ cup unsalted butter, melted
One 1-pound package phyllo, thawed if frozen

FOR SERVING

Confectioners' sugar ◆ Ground cinnamon

1 Make the filling. Pour the milk into a heavy saucepan and heat to just below a boil; remove from the heat.

2 Place the egg yolks and vanilla sugar (or sugar and vanilla extract) in a large bowl and, using a wire whisk or electric mixer, beat until pale and creamy. Whisk in the semolina, and gradually whisk in the hot milk. Rinse out the saucepan, return the custard mixture to it, and place over low heat. Cook, stirring constantly in a figure-eight motion with a wooden spoon, until firm enough to come away from the sides of the pan, about 5 minutes. Transfer to a large bowl. Secure the 1 tablespoon of butter on the tip of a knife and rub over the surface of the custard (this prevents a skin from forming). Lightly press waxed paper on top of the custard, and set aside to cool.

3 In a medium bowl, combine the cottage cheese and feta cheese. Cover tightly and refrigerate.

4 Make the syrup. Set a heavy saucepan over low-medium heat and add honey, sugar, water, lemon zest, and cinnamon stick. Bring to a boil. Simmer 10 minutes, or until the syrup coats the back of a metal spoon. Remove from the heat and set aside to cool slightly. Add the lemon juice and rose water.

5 Heat the oven to 350°F. Brush 2 baking trays with a little of the melted butter.

6 Using a metal spoon, combine the custard and cheese mixture. In another bowl, whisk egg whites until they hold stiff peaks; fold into the custard.

7 Divide the phyllo into 2 portions. Wrap 1 portion in plastic wrap and refrigerate. Lay the remaining sheets, stacked on top of each other, on the table, with the shorter side facing you. With a sharp knife, cut lengthwise in half. Stack these strips on top of each other.

8 Remove one strip from the pile and lay on a flat surface. Lightly brush with melted butter. Spread 3 tablespoons custard along the bottom of the strip, leaving a ¾-inch border along the lower edge and the sides. Fold the lower edge of the strip over the filling, and fold over twice. Bring the sides over the filling, lightly brush with butter, and gently fold up the strip to make a rectangle. Place seam side down on the baking tray. Continue until you have used up all the phyllo and filling. Space the pastries at least 2 inches apart on the baking tray and brush with the remaining melted butter. Bake 20 to 25 minutes or until crisp and golden.

9 Using a spatula, very carefully transfer the pies to one baking tray, packing them close together. Or transfer all the pies to a shallow dish that is large enough to hold them all in a single layer. While the pies are still hot, strain over all the syrup (discard the cinnamon stick and lemon zest). Lightly cover with a kitchen towel and set aside to cool.

10 Transfer the pies to a serving dish, spoon over some of the syrup, and generously dust with confectioners' sugar and cinnamon. Serve the rest of the syrup in a bowl.

Little Rice Puddings

Risogala

*When you make these little puddings, make a few more than you need—
they are a favorite any-time-of-day snack, as well as a lovely sweet treat
at the end of a meal. For a special occasion, flavor the puddings with
mastic, as my grandmother used to do.*

SERVES: 6

½ cup pudding rice or short-grained white rice ◆ 3 cups whole milk
1-inch piece of lemon zest from an unwaxed organic lemon
Pinch of salt to taste ◆ 1½ tablespoons unsalted butter
6 tablespoons superfine sugar or more to taste ◆ 2 egg yolks
½ teaspoon vanilla extract ◆ A few drops of freshly squeezed lemon juice
6 tablespoons light cream ◆ Ground cinnamon ◆ Confectioners' sugar

◆

1 Blanch the rice. Pour 2 inches water into a saucepan and bring to a boil. Stir in the rice and immediately remove the pan from the heat; drain.

2 Pour the milk into a heavy saucepan and bring to just under a boil. Add the rice, lemon zest, salt, butter, and 5 tablespoons sugar. Reduce the heat to very low. Stirring occasionally with a wooden spoon, simmer uncovered for 30 minutes or until thick and creamy but still moist. Remove the pan from the heat and set aside.

3 In a small bowl, whisk together the egg yolks, vanilla extract, and remaining 1 tablespoon sugar until pale and thick. Remove the lemon zest from the rice mixture and discard. Stir the egg mixture, lemon juice, and cream into the rice. Return the pan to very low heat and cook 2 minutes, stirring constantly with a wooden spoon. Taste, and add more sugar if desired. Divide between individual dishes, cover, and chill.

4 To serve, dust with cinnamon and confectioners' sugar to taste. To flavor the puddings with mastic, omit the vanilla extract and ground cinnamon. Pound ½ teaspoon mastic granules in a mortar with the remaining 1 tablespoon sugar. Add to the egg yolks and proceed as described in the recipe. Serve dusted only with confectioners' sugar.

Baklava

Baklavas

Baklavas is the perfect dessert for the cook who wants to enjoy her own party—not only is it straightforward to make, but you can make it one or two days in advance. Don't be put off by the quantities of butter and sugar in the recipe—baklavas is so rich that individual servings are very small.

MAKES: up to 24 pieces

SYRUP

1 cup Hymettus or other strongly flavored honey ◆ ½ cup superfine sugar
Zest of 1 small organic orange ◆ 1 cinnamon stick, broken into large pieces ◆ 1 cup water
2 tablespoons freshly squeezed lemon juice ◆ 2 tablespoons orange flower water (optional)

FILLING

3 cups finely chopped walnuts ◆ 1 cup finely chopped almonds
½ cup Hymettus or other strongly flavored honey ◆ 2 teaspoons ground cinnamon
Pinch of ground cloves ◆ ¾ cup unsalted butter, melted
One 1-pound package phyllo (at least 12 pastry sheets), thawed if frozen

◆

1 Heat the oven to 350°F.

2 Make the syrup. Place a syrup pan or heavy saucepan over low-medium heat and add the honey, sugar, orange zest, cinnamon stick, and water. Bring to a boil and simmer 10 minutes or until the syrup lightly coats the back of a metal spoon. Remove from the heat and set aside to cool slightly. Add the lemon juice and the orange flower water, if using.

3 Make the filling. In a small bowl, combine the walnuts, almonds, honey, cinnamon, and cloves.

4 Brush a 9- by 12-inch baking pan or cake pan, with sides at least 2½ inches deep, with melted butter (or choose a pan that fits the size of your phyllo sheets). Arrange 1 phyllo sheet in the pan, and brush with a little butter; repeat with two more sheets. Divide the filling into 4 portions. Very lightly, spread 1 portion over the phyllo

(avoid pressing down on the pastry). Cover with 1 phyllo sheet, brush with melted butter, and place another sheet on top. Brush this with butter, spread a second portion of filling over it, and repeat until filling and phyllo are used (ending with phyllo). Liberally brush with butter. With a small, sharp knife, carefully cut through (score) the top two phyllo sheets to make squares or diamond shapes.

5 Bake 40 minutes or until the top is golden brown. Immediately you remove the baklavas from the oven, use a sharp knife to cut into the shapes you have scored; cut through to the bottom of the pan. Strain over the syrup and discard the cinnamon stick and orange zest. Cover the pan with a clean kitchen towel and set aside for at least 4 hours.

◆

Honeyed Nuts and Cheese
Karythia Glykisma me Tyri

*Make this simple little treat when you can find some of our wonderfully thick,
rich Hymettus honey. Served alone or with any kind of fresh fruit,
this is the perfect end to a meal.*

SERVES: 6

**1 cup blanched almonds, cut lengthwise in halves ◆ 1 cup shelled walnuts
¾ cup Hymettus or orange blossom honey
6 slices manouri or aged graviera or pecorino cheese**

◆

1 Heat the oven to 325°F.

2 Spread the almonds and walnuts on a baking tray. Toast 10 minutes or until the almonds just begin to change color; set aside to cool.

3 Combine the nuts and honey in a serving bowl and set the bowl on a platter; arrange the cheese beside.

Almond Cake in Syrup

Revani

Syrupy revani is easy to make, and will keep in a covered container for several days. Serve it cut into squares or diamond shapes, with fresh fruit, myzithra or aged kephalotyri cheese, and Greek Coffee (see page 138).

MAKES: 15 to 20 servings

¾ cup superfine sugar ◆ 1½ cups water ◆ Zest and strained juice of 1 small organic lemon
1½ cups Hymettus or other strongly flavored honey
1 tablespoon unsalted butter, melted ◆ ½ cup unsalted butter ◆ 5 large eggs, separated
¾ cup fine-grain semolina ◆ ¾ cup ground almonds
½ teaspoon ground cinnamon ◆ 1 cup freshly squeezed orange juice, strained
¾ cup flaked blanched almonds

◆

1 Place a syrup pan or heavy saucepan over low-medium heat and add ½ cup of the sugar, the water, and the lemon zest. Bring to a boil and simmer 10 minutes. Add the honey and continue simmering until the syrup lightly coats the back of a metal spoon, about 5 minutes. Remove from the heat, and set aside to cool. Add the lemon juice.

2 Heat the oven to 350°F. Brush a 9-inch round or 7-inch square cake pan, at least 2½ inches deep, with the melted butter.

3 Place the butter and remaining sugar in a large bowl and, using a wire whisk or an electric mixer, beat together until white and fluffy.

Add the egg yolks, one at a time, beating constantly. With a spoon, stir in the semolina, ground almonds, cinnamon, and orange juice.

4 In a large bowl, whisk the egg whites until they form stiff peaks. With a metal spoon or spatula, stir one-third into the semolina mixture, then fold in the remainder. Pour into the cake pan, and sprinkle the flaked almonds on top. Bake 40 to 45 minutes or until pale golden brown and a cake tester is clean when removed.

5 As soon as you remove the cake from the oven, spoon on the syrup and zest; take care not to dislodge the almonds. Cover the pan with a kitchen towel and set aside for at least 2 hours.

Cherry Jam

Glyko Kerasi

This is more of a sweet on a spoon than a jam. We like to enjoy it when we need a little pick-me-up during the day (when we wake up from an afternoon nap, for instance), or with cheese at the end of a meal.

MAKES: About five 1-cup jars

6 cups dark, sweet cherries such as Morello
Juice of 2 small lemons ◆ 1½ pounds superfine sugar

1 Wash, sterilize, and thoroughly dry six 1-cup jars.

2 Pit the cherries and reserve 12 pits; crack these and remove the kernels. Tie the kernels in a piece of muslin to make a bag. Place this bag, the cherries, and lemon juice in a preserving pan, and place over low heat. Simmer, stirring occasionally to prevent sticking, until the cherries are very soft. Add the sugar and stir until dissolved. Raise the heat and boil rapidly until a candy thermometer reaches 221°F. If you don't have a candy thermometer, scoop up a little of the jam and drop onto a cold plate. It should begin to set almost immediately, and a thin skin should be visible when you gently push the jam with your finger.

3 Pour the jam into the jars. While still hot, cover the jam with waxed paper and tightly cover the jars. Store for up to 2 months.

Greek Coffee
Kafes

*To make coffee the same way we Greeks do, you will need a special piece of
equipment called a briki—a long-handled, small brass pot with a broad lip,
tapering toward the top (although you can make it very successfully in a small
saucepan, too). We use specially prepared coffee that is roasted and ground to a fine
powder, and we serve it in tiny cups. You can buy a briki, the coffee, and
traditional cups in Greek and Middle Eastern stores.*
*When we sweeten our coffee, we do so in the pot. Therefore, you will need to know
how your guests take their coffee—without sugar (sketo), with some sugar
(metrio), or sweet (glyko). With luck, they will all want it made to the same degree
of sweetness. Otherwise, you will have to make separate pots. Serve with tall
glasses of iced water.*

SERVES: 4

4 coffee cups water ◆ **4 teaspoons powder-fine (Greek) ground coffee, heaped to taste**
4 teaspoons sugar, heaped to taste

◆

1 Bring the water to a boil in a 4- to 6-cup briki
(or small saucepan). Remove from the heat and
sprinkle the coffee and sugar over the water; stir
once or twice. Bring to a boil again, and remove
from the heat. Stir until the froth has disappeared,
and return to the heat; repeat this once more.
(This process is necessary for thick coffee.)

2 Divide the froth between the cups (it will
bring good luck!) and carefully pour in the
coffee to the brim. The froth will rise to the
surface. Serve at once.

Sage Tea
Faskomilo

This is the tea I make whenever someone isn't feeling as well as they should. The nearby mountains are covered in sage (salvia fructicosa, a more aromatic member of the same botanical family as garden sage, salvia officinalis). We rarely use it in cooking, but we love our sage tea. If you have sage in your garden, pick it in sprigs, just before it flowers, tie the sprigs together, and hang this bundle somewhere dry and warm. Properly dried, sage can be kept for months. When you feel the unwelcome symptoms of a cold or flu, or when you have an upset stomach or just feel in need of a little tender loving care, try our sage tea.

SERVES: 4

4 large sprigs dried sage or 8 tablespoons dried sage leaves ♦ 4 glasses water
4 teaspoons Hymettus or other strongly flavored honey

♦

1 Combine the sage and water in a saucepan and slowly bring to a boil. Rinse 4 glasses in hot water to warm them. Strain the tea into the glasses and stir 1 teaspoon honey into each one.

Mama says...
We attribute great powers to our sage tea, but we like other herb teas (tsai) too—chamomile (kamomili) for a relaxing nighttime tea, mint (thiosmos) when a fever threatens, thyme (thimari) for a sore chest, and for a special pick-me-up, Cretan dittany (dictamos).

FESTIVALS

Easter

Easter, our most important and most festive holiday, is a wonderful time of year for us. To mark the end of weeks of austerity and the beginning of a time of abundance, we celebrate by spit-roasting or oven-baking a milk-fed lamb or kid. Everyone helps in the preparation of the Easter midday feast. The atmosphere is one of great joy—the family is at the table, and we look forward to another year together.

In the village, the week preceding Easter is always one of frantic activity—the animals have to be slaughtered and prepared, the baker works overtime as he makes our beautiful Easter breads, my kitchen overflows with cookies, and our house is whitewashed in preparation for the summer heat.

The Easter feast really begins in the early hours of Easter Sunday, when we arrive home from midnight mass. Breaking our long Lent fast, we have a meal of mayeritsa soup (made from lamb innards), Easter bread, and salad. This helps prepare our stomachs for the rich food that awaits us later that day.

Our Easter feast begins with mezes of kokkoretsi (lamb innards), olives, and fresh cheese. The Easter lamb follows, and it is served with a Romaine Lettuce Salad (see page 80), Easter bread, and the best spring vegetables I can find. We finish with delectable little sweet cheese pies and Easter cookies, then we take to our beds for a few hours rest!

Easter Lamb
Arnaki Paskalino Psito

For our Easter feast, we have only milk-fed lamb. But this is not so easy to find away from our countryside, even for Greeks. The recipe here is for the more available spring lamb, which is larger and has a little more fat than the milk-fed lamb.

SERVES: 6

One 3- to 4-pound leg of lamb, trimmed of excess fat ◆ Juice of 2 large lemons ½ cup extra-virgin olive oil ◆ Coarse sea salt and finely cracked pepper to taste 2 tablespoons dried Greek oregano ◆ 6 sprigs of rosemary ◆ ½ cup dry red wine ½ cup meat broth or water ◆ 6 large potatoes suitable for roasting, cut lengthwise into large pieces

◆

1 Heat the oven to 400°F.

2 With your hand, rub the lamb with the juice of 1 lemon, 4 tablespoons of the olive oil, salt, pepper, and 1 tablespoon oregano. Place in a heavy roasting pan or baking dish, sprinkle the rosemary on top, and add the wine and half the broth (or water) to the dish. Bake uncovered for 20 minutes; baste once or twice.

3 Add the remaining broth to the dish, reduce the oven temperature to 350°F, and bake 15 (for a smaller leg) to 30 minutes (for a larger leg).

Remove the dish from the oven. Arrange the potatoes around the meat and turn once to baste. Sprinkle the potatoes with the rest of the olive oil and oregano, and salt and pepper to taste. Bake 40 minutes longer; baste once or twice. Remove a spoonful of pan juices and combine with the remaining lemon juice. Pour this sauce over the potatoes and bake 20 minutes or until the potatoes are browned.

4 Cut the meat into slices and arrange on a warm platter with the potatoes. Serve the pan juices separately.

Red Eggs
Avga Kokkina

A large bowl of red eggs is at the center of our Easter celebrations. They signify both the rebirth and the blood of Christ, and we each take one to midnight mass on Easter Saturday. As the bells ring out Easter morning, we turn to each other in church and, with the words, "Christ is risen," we tap our egg against that of the person next to us. After our breakfast at home, we retire to bed exhausted but happy, in anticipation of the next day's feast. Unlike real Easter eggs, red eggs are never eaten.

12 white eggs, at room temperature (check that they have not been waxed or oiled)
4 teaspoons red food coloring ♦ ½ teaspoon blue food coloring ♦ 2 tablespoons olive oil

♦

1 Half fill a large, stainless steel saucepan with water. Bring to a boil and add the food coloring. Gently lower the eggs into the water, and lightly boil 20 minutes; add a little more coloring if necessary to produce deep crimson eggs.

2 Remove the pan from the heat and let the eggs cool in the water. Remove with a slotted spoon and set aside to dry. Dip a paper towel in the olive oil and rub each egg all over with the oil.

Mama says...
Red eggs are baked into the almond-topped bread, which is rich in butter and eggs (foods forbidden during Lent), that we eat to break the Lenten fast. Other loaves, all of which display our village baker's artistry, are decorated with symbols of rebirth—flowers, leaves, and berries—shaped in dough. Many of our baker's Easter breads are so beautifully crafted that we use them as wall decorations throughout the year.

Sweet Cheese Pies
Skaltsounia

*Some of the best moments I spend before our Easter celebration are those when
I make these delightful little pastries. My neighbors are doing the same in their
kitchens, and we all love to compare (and, out of earshot, criticize!) each other's
skaltsounia over coffee and a chat. In our village, we use fresh myzithra cheese
for the filling. But it's not easy to find elsewhere, even in Athens, so I give a useful
substitute here. You can make the pies all one shape or, for a really attractive table,
you can make different shapes—triangles, squares, and rolls. Serve with bowls of
warm Hymettus or orange blossom honey.*

MAKES: approximately 24 pastries

FILLING
1¼ cups unsalted butter, melted
2 cups cottage cheese, drained and pressed through a strainer
⅓ cup feta cheese, drained and finely grated ♦ 2 egg yolks, lightly beaten
⅜ cup Hymettus or other strongly flavored honey ♦ 1 teaspoon vanilla extract
1 teaspoon ground cinnamon ♦ 2 tablespoons brandy (optional)
One 1-pound package phyllo, thawed if frozen

FOR SERVING
Orange flower water ♦ Sifted confectioners' sugar ♦ Bowls of honey

♦

1 Heat the oven to 350°F. Brush 2 baking trays with a little of the melted butter.

2 Make the filling. In a medium bowl, lightly mash the cottage cheese and feta cheese together. Add the egg yolks, honey, vanilla extract, cinnamon, and brandy if using, and mash lightly with a fork until well mixed but not smooth. Set aside.

3 Divide the phyllo into 2 portions. Wrap 1 portion in plastic wrap and refrigerate.

4 Divide the remaining sheets in half; fold 1 portion in half and loosely cover with plastic wrap; set aside. Lay the remaining sheets, stacked on top of each other, on the table, with the shorter side facing you.

5 To make triangles: Cut the phyllo sheets lengthwise into 3 strips and stack the strips on top of each other. Remove the top strip from the pile and lightly brush with melted butter. Place a second strip on top of the first, and lightly brush that one also. Place 2 tablespoons of the filling on the bottom end of the buttered strips. Take the bottom right corner of both strips between finger and thumb and fold over to the left side to make a triangle. Gently pull up the bottom left corner and fold up to make a second triangle. Continue folding until you reach the top. Place seam side down on the baking tray, spaced 1 inch apart. Repeat with the remaining phyllo and filling.

To make rolls: Cut the phyllo sheets lengthwise into 2 strips and stack on top of each other.

Remove the top strip from the pile and lightly brush with melted butter. Place a second strip on top of the first, and lightly brush that one also. Spread 2 tablespoons of the filling along the bottom of the strip, leaving a ¾-inch border along the lower edge and the sides. Fold the lower edges of the strips over the filling and roll over twice. Bring both sides over the filling, lightly brush with butter, and roll up the strip. Place seam side down on the baking tray, spaced 1 inch apart. Repeat with all the remaining phyllo and filling.

To make rectangles: Make as rolls, but fold into rectangles instead.

6 Brush the pies with the remaining melted butter and bake 20 to 25 minutes or until crisp and golden.

7 Stack the pies on a serving plate, sprinkle with orange blossom water, and generously dust with confectioners' sugar. Serve with bowls of honey.

Mama says...
Whenever I make feta cheese I use the leftover whey (water) to make mizythra. I line a small basket with muslin and stand this on a tray, so the cheese can drain. I add some fresh milk to the whey, then pour this into the basket. When it has settled, I cover the cheese and weight it. After a day or two, I turn out the cheese onto a plate.

CHRISTMAS AND NEW YEAR

Christmas and the New Year are the times we like to spend visiting family and friends. Christmas isn't quite so important in our year as it is in other Christian calendars, but we still like to make special cakes and breads for the occasion. It is a time of year when we don't work quite so hard, so we can spend those short, dark days enjoying some wonderful sweet treats.

New Year Cake
Vassilopitta

When we return from church on New Year's Day we always make a ceremony of cutting vassilopitta. I bake an old silver coin in it; whoever finds the coin in their slice of bread will not only receive good fortune the entire year, but can also keep the coin! Like many of my neighbors, I make vassilopitta (without the coin) throughout the year. I make it in the shape of a long loaf, for easy storing. More a sweet bread than a cake, it's wonderful toasted for breakfast, and I like a slice with jam in the afternoon. It will keep several days in an airtight container, and also freezes well.

MAKES: 1 large, round cake or 2 loaves

1 cup plus 2 tablespoons milk, heated to tepid (110°F)
2 tablespoons active dry yeast ◆ 7 to 9 cups all-purpose flour
7 eggs ◆ ¾ cup honey ◆ 1 teaspoon fine sea salt or to taste
⅔ cup superfine sugar ◆ ¾ cup unsalted butter, melted ◆ 5 tablespoons olive oil
2 tablespoons finely grated orange zest, briefly dried in a low oven,
and pulverized in a mortar with 1 teaspoon sugar
¾ cup sesame seeds

◆

1 Pour 1 cup milk into a medium bowl, add the yeast, and set aside 10 minutes in a warm spot or until foamy.

2 Using a wooden spoon, stir 1 cup of the flour into the yeast. Tightly cover the bowl and set aside in a warm, draft-free spot for 1 hour or until spongelike in texture.

3 Break 6 eggs into a large bowl and add the honey, salt, and all but 2 teaspoons of the sugar. Using a wire whisk or electric mixer, beat until light and frothy.

4 Sift 6 cups flour into another large bowl and make a well in the center. Pour in the yeast sponge, ½ cup melted butter, 4 tablespoons olive oil, the orange zest, and the egg mixture. Knead 5 minutes, transfer to a lightly floured surface, and knead 10 minutes longer; add enough of the remaining flour to make a soft, smooth dough.

5 Wipe the inside of a large bowl with half the remaining oil and place the dough in it; brush with the remaining olive oil. Tightly cover the bowl with plastic wrap. Set aside in a warm draft-free spot for 2 hours or until the dough is at least doubled in bulk.

6 Transfer to a lightly floured surface and knead 5 minutes. Liberally butter a baking tray or 2 loaf tins with the remaining butter. Form the dough into a round 2-inch-thick cake and flatten the top slightly with your palm, or divide into 2 portions and place in the loaf tins. Using a wooden skewer or equivalent, write the year on top of the cake for a New Year celebration, or make a simple design on the loaves. Loosely cover with plastic wrap, and set aside for 30 minutes in a warm, draft-free spot.

7 Heat the oven to 375°F. In a small bowl, beat the remaining egg with the reserved 2 teaspoons sugar and the 2 tablespoons milk. Liberally brush the cake or loaves with this glaze and sprinkle with sesame seeds. Bake 40 to 50 minutes or until deep chestnut brown. Cool on a rack.

Mama says...
Vassilopitta, or St Basil's bread, is special because Saint Basil is one of the most important saints in the Orthodox church. The name, vassilikos, or basil, means "kingly," and we have the same high regard for the herb of that name as we do for the bread.

Honey Syrup Cakes
Melomacarona

I offer these lovely, sweet, sticky cakes to all who visit us over Christmas and the New Year. Melomacarona may be stored in an airtight container for up to one week.

MAKES: 24 small cakes

CAKES
½ cup unsalted butter, melted ◆ ½ cup olive oil, plus more if needed
¾ cup fine semolina ◆ 2 tablespoons superfine sugar
2 tablespoons finely grated zest of an organic orange, briefly dried in a low oven and
pulverized in a mortar with 1 teaspoon sugar ◆ 2 tablespoons brandy
½ cup Hymettus or other strongly flavored honey
1¼ to 1¾ cups all-purpose flour ◆ 1 scant teaspoon baking powder
¼ teaspoon grated nutmeg ◆ ½ teaspoon ground cloves

SYRUP
1 cup Hymettus or other strongly flavored honey ◆ 1½ cups water
Strained juice of 1 small lemon
Strained juice of 1 small orange or 2 tablespoons orange flower water

FOR SERVING
1 cup shelled walnuts, finely chopped ◆ 1 teaspoon ground cinnamon
3 tablespoons superfine sugar

◆

1 Heat the oven to 350°F. Brush 2 baking trays with the 2 tablespoons melted butter.

2 Make the cakes. In a large bowl, combine the remaining butter and the olive oil. Gradually stir in the semolina, sugar, orange zest, brandy, and honey.

3 Sift together 1¼ cups of the flour, the baking powder, nutmeg, and cloves into a bowl; stir into the semolina mixture. Turn out onto a lightly floured surface and knead 10 minutes or until soft and pliant. If the dough seems stiff, add a little more oil; if thin, add more flour.

4 Form the dough into egg-sized ovals and set 2 inches apart on the baking trays. With the back of a fork, lightly press down twice on top of each oval to make a crisscross design, slightly flattening them at the same time. Bake 20 minutes or until lightly browned. Transfer to a rack to cool.

5 While the cakes are cooling, make the syrup: Place a syrup pan or heavy saucepan over low heat and add the honey and water. Bring to a boil and simmer 4 minutes. Remove the pan from the heat and add the lemon juice and orange juice (or orange flower water).

6 Using a spoon, place the barely warm cakes in the hot syrup, a few at a time. Leave in the syrup for 1 minute, and transfer to paper cake cases or to a serving platter. Combine the walnuts, cinnamon, and sugar, and sprinkle over the cakes.

Mama says...
When my mother told me that honey was "magical," I always believed her. She used honey all the time—in cakes and pies, to sweeten my drinks, and in all kinds of baked goods. She even used to smear it on wounds when I fell over. This same magical quality works for my own family now. Our best Greek honey is from Mount Hymettus, where the bees feed on the pollen of wild thyme flowers, but our citrus blossom honey and sage honeys are wonderful too.

Almond Shortcakes

Kourabiedes

At the center of all my festive tables is a platter piled high with snowy white, sugar-dusted shortcakes called kourabiedes. Lightly scented with rose water, these buttery treats are perfect with Cherry Jam (see page 137) or fresh fruit. I find that their flavor improves if they are kept a day or two in an airtight container. To store them, generously sprinkle confectioners' sugar over each layer of shortcakes, and dust with fresh confectioners' sugar just before serving.

MAKES: about 36 shortcakes

2 cups unsalted butter, at room temperature ◆ ½ cup superfine sugar
1 teaspoon vanilla extract ◆ 2 tablespoons brandy ◆ 2 large eggs, separated
1½ cups ground almonds ◆ 2½ to 2¾ cups all-purpose flour
½ teaspoon baking powder ◆ 2 tablespoons unsalted butter, melted
3 tablespoons rose water (available in specialty food stores)
1⅔ cups confectioners' sugar

◆

1 Place the room-temperature butter in a large bowl and, using an electric mixer or wooden spoon, beat until light and fluffy. Beat in the sugar, vanilla extract, brandy, and egg yolks.

2 In a second large bowl, whisk the egg whites until thick. Add to the butter mixture with the ground almonds and mix well. Sift in half the flour and the baking powder, and beat to mix. With your fingers, gradually mix in enough of the remaining flour to make a soft dough. Tightly cover the bowl and refrigerate 1 hour.

3 Heat the oven to 325°F. Lightly brush 2 baking trays with the melted butter, and dust with flour.

4 Break off pieces of dough the size of very small eggs and shape into ovals, pears, or crescents. Arrange 2 inches apart on the baking trays. Bake 15 to 20 minutes or until firm and very pale gold. Transfer to racks to cool.

5 Sprinkle the shortcakes with rose water. Spread a generous layer of confectioners' sugar on a plate and pile the shortcakes on top, liberally dusting each layer with sugar.

NAME DAYS AND OTHER CELEBRATIONS

We don't celebrate birthdays in the same way as most other people. Instead we celebrate the day of the saint that we are named for (almost all Greeks are named after a saint). We are even entitled to a day off work to enjoy the occasion. This can, however, pose problems, as it has long been customary to name the firstborn son George. With so many Georges in the country, Saint George's day has almost become a national holiday! It's a rather nice custom for children though, as they can have big communal parties on their Name Day and take the day off from school, as well.

Our years are also marked by baptisms, weddings, and the visits of relatives who are returning to the village from far-off countries. Of course, we have a host of other excuses for celebrations, too. During all of these festivals, our most treasured foods are the delightful sweet treats that we Greeks love so much.

Pistachio and Sesame Brittle
Pasteli

When we celebrate a Name Day in our house, we like to have plenty of little pastries and candies on hand, as almost the entire village stops by (several times!) on the day. This is our favorite candy, and it's one that has a very long history in our country. It is also very, very good crushed and sprinkled over ice cream.

MAKES: at least 24 pieces

1¾ cups sesame seeds ◆ ½ cup superfine sugar ◆ ¼ cup water ◆ 1⅛ cups Hymettus or other strongly flavored honey ◆ 3 tablespoons freshly squeezed lemon juice
1¼ cups unsalted pistachio nuts, coarsely chopped ◆ 2 tablespoons unsalted butter, melted
1 tablespoon orange flower water (optional)

◆

1 Lightly toast the sesame seeds. Either spread on a dry baking tray and bake in a low oven for 5 minutes, shaking the tray once or twice, or set a dry heavy skillet or frying pan over low heat and toast 3 to 4 minutes, occasionally shaking the skillet to prevent scorching.

2 Put the sugar and water in a small, heavy saucepan set over low heat; slowly bring to a boil. Add the honey, bring back to a boil, and simmer until the mixture reaches the soft ball stage (235 to 240°F) on a candy thermometer (or drop a small quantity of the candy into a glass of cold water—if it forms a wobbly ball, it's ready). Add the lemon juice, pistachio nuts, and sesame seeds, and stir well with a wooden spoon to mix. Continue stirring over low heat for 1 minute.

3 Line a jelly roll pan or baking tray with waxed paper and brush with melted butter. Pour in the pasteli and, using a spatula, spread to make a ½-inch layer. Sprinkle with orange flower water (if using), and set aside 15 minutes to cool a little.

4 While the pasteli is still warm, use a sharp knife to score (cut) into squares or strips (this helps you break it into pieces later). Lightly cover the pan with a kitchen towel and set aside to cool completely (or leave overnight).

5 To remove the pasteli, turn the pan upside down and peel off the paper. Using a small, sharp knife, cut into pieces along the score marks you have made. Store between layers of waxed paper in an airtight container for up to 2 weeks.

Nut Pastries in Honey Syrup
Amigdalota

The filling in these pastries is heady with cinnamon and cloves, lovely spices we remember long after our celebrations. I make amigdalota in the shape of half-moons or pretty little squares. Sometimes I fry them, but I prefer to bake them, as I can make larger quantities at one time.

MAKES: approximately 24 pastries

FILLING
2 egg whites ◆ 2½ cups unsalted, skinned pistachio nuts, walnuts, or blanched almonds or a mixture, chopped ◆ ½ teaspoon ground cloves ◆ 1 teaspoon ground cinnamon
½ cup Hymettus or other strongly flavored honey

PIE DOUGH
2¼ cups all-purpose flour plus 4 tablespoons ◆ Pinch of fine sea salt
1 tablespoon finely grated lemon zest, briefly dried in a low oven and pulverized in a mortar with 1 teaspoon sugar ◆ ½ cup unsalted butter, cold, cut into small pieces
2 egg whites ◆ 1 teaspoon vanilla extract ◆ 1 to 3 tablespoons cold milk or water
4 tablespoons unsalted butter, melted
2 egg yolks lightly beaten with 2 tablespoons water

SYRUP
1 cup Hymettus or other strongly flavored honey ◆ ½ cup superfine sugar
Zest of 1 organic lemon, removed in thin strips ◆ 1 cup water ◆ Juice of ½ lemon
2 tablespoons rose water or orange flower water (optional)

FOR SERVING
Sifted confectioners' sugar
¾ cup finely chopped unsalted pistachio nuts, walnuts, or blanched almonds

1 Make the filling. Beat the egg whites in a large bowl until they hold soft peaks. Add the nuts, cloves, cinnamon, and honey, and lightly stir to mix; set aside.

2 Make the pie dough. Sift the flour into a large bowl and stir in the salt and lemon zest. Add the butter, and lightly rub the mixture together with your fingers until it resembles coarse bread crumbs. In a medium bowl, whisk the egg whites until they just hold soft peaks. Add the flour with the vanilla and knead well, adding milk (or water) if necessary to make a smooth and elastic dough. Tightly cover the dough with plastic wrap and refrigerate 1 hour.

3 Heat the oven to 350°F. Lightly brush 2 baking trays or cookie sheets with melted butter.

4 Divide the dough in half, rewrap 1 portion in plastic wrap, and return this to the refrigerator. Scatter the remaining 4 tablespoons flour over a clean work surface and roll out the pie dough as thin as possible. Use a 4-inch round cutter or inverted glass to cut into circles, or use a small, sharp knife to cut 4-inch squares. Place 1 heaping tablespoon filling in the centers of each circle. Dip your finger in water and lightly dampen the pie dough edges; fold in half to make half-moons. Crimp the edges with a pastry wheel or fork to seal, or pull the corners of each square almost into the center to make a smaller square with a little filling exposed; lightly press the edges together. Arrange the pastries 1 inch apart on the baking trays. Repeat with the remaining pie dough and filling. Brush with the remaining butter and bake 15 minutes or until the pie dough is firm.

5 Brush the pastries with the beaten egg yolks and bake 10 minutes longer or until golden brown. Cool on a rack.

6 While the pastries are baking, make the syrup. Set a syrup pan or small, heavy saucepan over low heat and add the honey, sugar, lemon zest, and water. Bring to a boil and simmer 10 minutes or until the syrup lightly coats the back of a metal spoon. Set aside to cool slightly. Add the lemon juice and rose (or orange flower) water.

7 Dip the hot pastries into the warm syrup, a few at a time, and pile on a serving platter. Sprinkle with confectioners' sugar and nuts, and serve warm or cold. Serve any remaining syrup in a bowl.

Glossary

Briki: A long-handled small brass pot with a broad lip, tapering towards the top, used to make Greek coffee.

Cannellini beans: White haricot beans, usually available canned or dried, used in soups, stews, and salads.

Chickpeas: Dried chickpeas are used extensively in the Mediterranean. Ground chickpea flour is blended with ordinary flour for a nutty flavor.

Cilantro: Cilantro is a herb native to the Eastern Mediterranean and has been cultivated there since ancient times.

Currants: Named for the ancient Greek city of Corinth which gained great wealth from the trading of currants, these tiny dried grapes are packed with valuable nutrients.

Dolmades: Grape leaves usually wrapped around rice and herbs and flavored with meat or vegetables to make parcels. Grape leaves are available bottled in brine. Dolmadakia are small dolmades.

Feta cheese: A crumbly, salty cheese made from sheep's milk and cured in brine. Still made using traditional methods, feta can be eaten in salads or simply sprinkled with a little olive oil and dried Greek oregano.

Flower waters: Orange flower water and rose water are used in Mediterranean cuisine to impart fragrance to desserts such as rice puddings and custards. They are usually sprinkled over the dessert or stirred in just before serving.

Fricassée: A stew of white meat, such as chicken, rabbit, or veal, in which the meat and vegetables are gently sautéed in olive oil, then cooked in stock, and finished with eggs.

Garlic: Awarded almost magical properties by doctors in Greek antiquity, garlic is used in *skorthalia* (a sauce made from pounded garlic and nuts), and in meat and fish dishes.

Hilopites: Tiny, square Greek pasta.

Honey: Since time immemorial, honey has been a staple of Greek food culture. It is healthful, versatile, and a good alternative to sugar. Hymettus honey, which the Greeks consider the best, is clear, thick, and infused with thyme.

Horta: Wild herbs and greens.

Kasseri: A Greek cheese reconstituted from the curds of Kephalotyri. It can be grated and sprinkled on *macaronia*.

Kephalotyri: A hard Greek cheese made from unpasteurized sheep's or goat's milk. It is particularly good fried.

Kephtedes: Large rissoles or patties made with minced meat or vegetables. Kephtedakia are small kephtedes.

Lathera: A dish of vegetables of choice, cooked slowly in a sauce of olive oil, onions, tomatoes, and seasonings.

Lovage: A perennial herb used in salads and cooking, and similar to celery leaves.

Macaronia: Greek pasta

Mastic: A natural resin, native to the Eastern Mediterranean and used to flavor sweet dishes and drinks.

Mavrodaphne: *Mavrodaphne* grapes grow around Patras and make for a dessert wine similar to port.

Meze: Greek appetizers or starter dishes, usually served as a selection.

Moustalevria: Jelly-like sweet made from petimezi.

Myzithra: A soft cheese made by adding fresh sheep's or goat's milk to the whey from *feta* or *kephalotyri*.

Okra: Green seed pods used in cooked dishes, also known as lady's fingers.

Olive oil, extra-virgin: Oil from the first cold pressing of the olives, particularly low in acidity and therefore perfect in salads.

Olives: Olives are grown throughout the Mediterranean. Ripe black and under-ripe green olives are cured in seasoned brines, oils, and vinegars according to regional preferences. Amfissa, Thasos, or Atalanti olives are Greek varieties. Kalamata olives are a specialty of the Peloponnese.

Orzo: Greek pasta.

Ouzo: A strong Greek spirit flavored with aniseed and drunk with water.

Parsley: Flat-leaf parsley is a hugely popular herb in Greek cooking, with its mild flavor and health benefits.

Petimezi: New wine made before the grape juice has fermented.

Pine nuts: Native to Greece, with a delicate flavor that complements pilafs.

Plaki: Layered, baked dishes.

Purslane: A wild herb used in salads.

Quinces: In Greek legend, quinces were associated with love, fertility, and marriage—it was a golden quince that Paris presented to Aphrodite, sparking the Trojan War.

Retsina: Traditionally, the Greeks store their wine in airtight jars with clay and resin, hence the unique taste of retsina.

Rigani: Greek oregano which grows wild in the Mediterranean, with a stronger flavor than Italian oregano. Fresh or dried, it is widely used in Greek salads, pasta, and grilled meats.

Rigatoni: Short, hollow pasta tubes.

Salates: Dips.

Saganaki: A two-handled frying pan, it lends its name to a fried cheese dish.

Samos wine: A smooth, sweet Muscat wine from the island of Samos.

Stifado: A meat or seafood dish with the same quantity of small, whole onions as meat.

Sumac: A spice from the Mediterranean shrub of the same name.

Tahini: A paste made from ground toasted sesame seeds.

Tapsi: A round baking pan.

Trachanas: A Greek pasta made from soured sheep's milk.

Yogurt, strained: Used in tsatsiki and other dishes.

Index

Mama says...
Kitchen life is controlled by the seasons—create dishes from whatever vegetables are available that day.